FOLK EROTICA

FOLK

EROTICA

Celebrating Centuries of Erotic Americana

Milton Simpson

HarperCollinsPublishers

HarperCollins books may be purchased for educational, business, or sales promotional use. For information, please write: Special Markets Department, HarperCollins Publishers, Inc., 10 East 53rd Street, New York, NY 10022.

FIRST EDITION

Designed and produced by Johnson & Simpson Graphic Designers

LIBRARY OF CONGRESS CATALOGING-IN-PUBLICATION DATA

Simpson, Milton, 1930–
Folk erotica/by Milton Simpson.—1st ed.
 p. cm.
Includes bibliographical references and index.
ISBN 0-06-017108-1
1. Erotic art—Catalogs. 2. Popular culture—Catalogs.
I. Title.
N8217.E6S54 1994
704.9′ 428—dc20   94-25800

94 95 96 97 98   10 9 8 7 6 5 4 3 2 1

CONTENTS

6   INTRODUCTION

8   A GLOBAL HISTORY OF EROTICA

10   PRE-NINETEENTH CENTURY

24   THE NINETEENTH CENTURY

56   THE TWENTIETH CENTURY

142 SELECTED BIBLIOGRAPHY

143 INDEX

Historical essays and captions by Jenifer P. Borum

This book is about sex, America's notions of sex and sexuality as depicted and manifested in its folk art and artifacts. It's about orifices and phalluses. It's about fun. It encompasses works from early Native American culture, where sex was part of ritual, nature, education, and the spiritual, as well as pieces from a puritanical society, where sex was hidden, disguised, and censored, and explores the twentieth century, revealing what has changed and what hasn't.

Is the material presented in this book erotic or pornographic? I believe that one person's erotica is another's pornography. America has always been ambivalent in the face of erotic art, dismissing most erotica with disgust as pornography. While sexuality has been an important factor in the global context of world art and while the aesthetics and sensuality of the human body have played central roles in the development of Western art, censorship has been imposed in America. Scholars and museums have given little recognition to the subject. One of the few exceptions is Gerson Legman, the world's foremost authority on erotic folklore, who said: "Sex and its folklore are far more interesting, more valuable and more important in every social and historical sense than, for instance. . . murder, cruelty, torture, treachery."

But how do folk art, self-taught, naive art, and Americana enter into this debate? It is not the purview of this book or my own expertise to enter the nonmainstream definition controversy. So I leave that to scholars of art, folklore, anthropology, psychology, and history. The term *folk* is used liberally here, as the purpose of the survey within is to celebrate the wealth of nonmainstream American erotica, rather than to bandy about definitions. Louis C. Jones, a pioneer researcher and educator, in his introduction to *How to Know American Folk Art,* said: "It

really doesn't matter what we call it; it exists item by item and should be enjoyed for its own sake. We should not casually pass over this point, for folk art is to be enjoyed; it was created to make life less dreary, and it still so functions."

Erotic art, and the appreciation thereof, has been the life work for the husband-and-wife team of psychologists Drs. Phyllis and Eberhard Kronhausen. They have authored books, documentary films, and exhibitions, and began a crusade in the late fifties to change the way society viewed sex, from something forbidden and dirty to something natural and worthy of celebration.

Lawrence Ernst Gichner (1907–1992), like the Kronhausens, was a pioneer in the field of sexuality, particularly as it has been expressed in Oriental art, and like the Kronhausens, he suffered for his beliefs and activities in America. Gichner was persecuted by the U.S. government during the fifties simply for sending chapters from his planned book, which contained sexually explicit illustrations, through the mail.

Until now, only one book, *Eros du Dimanche (Erotic Art of Sunday Painters),* published in Paris in 1964, has taken up the subject of erotic folk art. Unfortunately, few American pieces were included in that work. I intend for this book to fill that gap.

The works presented here are linked by three unmistakable traits—the American experience, nonacademic ingenuity, and a celebration of human sexuality. The bases for the selection of the material for inclusion were: the best possible quality, variety within the book's format, an appeal to the widest possible audience—women as well as men—and a balance between explicit and nonexplicit material. In my research, I discovered recurring themes: action toys, coffin art, sailors' items, workers' off-hours creations, prisoners' art, and unusual media such as tattoos and graffiti, as well as painting and sculpture. Also, no collecting categories were spared—birdhouses, militaria, tools (both industrial and kitchen accessories), glass, pottery, and sports pieces.

This book is an overview of erotic Americana and is designed to provoke, inform, entertain, amuse, excite, and uplift as wide an audience as possible. A feast of visual excitement, this book will shed a little light on a broad and provocative subject.

The origin of this work is a fortuitous combination of two events. Event number one: Rod Lich and Susan Parrett were kind enough to share a few pieces from their collection of American erotica with me. Event number two: After a gestation period of two days, I phoned Herbert Waide Hemphill, Jr., who, because of his pioneering book *Twentieth-Century American Folk Art and Artists* published in 1974, is now considered the major source on the subject. I asked if a book had ever been produced on the subject of erotic American folk art. His answer was "No, they wouldn't dare."

My next question was "Do you feel the material warrants a book?" I received the answer I was hoping to hear: "Definitely." I was truly elated. "Mr. American Folk Art" was exhorting me to go for it! Bert also consented to have some pieces from his collection included in the project. My question, a gnawing question addressed to him, was "How do I track down other examples, enough material to fill this book?" I knew that Bert was a man of few words, but the answer I elicited prompted a sinking feeling in me. It was just one word: "Dig." What manner of wise counsel was that?

Bert Hemphill—you're magnificent! You were absolutely right. I have done some digging, much more than can be included in this book, and know that there is still more digging to do. Hopefully, other works on the subject will follow. The book's organization begins with an historical erotic time line, followed by a division of three sections, pre–nineteenth century, nineteenth century, and twentieth century. The sequence of material within each section is determined by both chronological and visual considerations. I hope you enjoy these images.

ACKNOWLEDGMENTS

The production of this book is the result of the efforts and dedication of many individuals. I am particularly grateful to the many private collectors (both named and anonymous), art dealers, public museums, and institutions who shared their examples and expertise with us. In a very small way the on-page credits acknowledge them. A special note of gratitude to Todd Smith, associate curator of the Kinsey Institute for Research in Sex, Gender and Reproduction. He made my research trip to Bloomington, Indiana, worthwhile. My gratitude to Arne Anton, Seymour Chwast, Cathleen Gallander, and C.J. Scheiner, whose counsel was invaluable.

The book's emphasis is primarily visual, but the three insightful essays and extended captions written by Jenifer Borum with scholarship and verve illuminate the material and place it into an historical and societal context.

At Johnson & Simpson, many thanks to Jeffrey Kibler for his wonderful contribution to the design and for keeping on top of all the facets in the production of this book. His wonderful line drawings beautifully enhance the time line on the next spread. Thanks also to Connie Johnson for working diligently at the studio on the book's many and often challenging details.

I am also grateful to Eamon Dolan, my editor at HarperCollins, for his support from the start and throughout the process of producing this book.

Milton Simpson

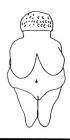    

Europe (prehistoric) Paleolithic: *Venus of Willendorf,* c. 5000 B.C.–3500 B.C.

Greece (classical): *Vase Painting,* 480 B.C.–323 B.C.

Peru (pre-Columbian, Moche, 1525 B.C.–1000 B.C.): *Ceramic Pottery,* 600 B.C.–200 B.C.

Rome (510 B.C.–A.D. 330): *Bronze Mirror,* 1st century A.D.

America (prehistoric: Native American, Southwest, 1000 B.C.–A.D. 1492): Fremont Petroglyphs, A.D. 950–1200

8

Italy (renaissance, 1250–1550): Giulio Romano, *The Loves of the Gods,* 1524

Japan (from A.D. 700): *Shunga,* 1660–1860

Flanders (baroque, 1625–1700): Peter Paul Rubens, *Leda and the Swan,* c. 1630

Italy (baroque, 1600–1770): Gian Bernini, *The Ecstasy of Saint Theresa,* 1645–1652

England (18th century): Thomas Rowlandson, *Untitled Watercolor,* c. 1790

England (late 19th century): Aubrey Beardsley, *The Examination of the Herald,* 1896

America (Native American, Pawnee, 19th century): Catlinite Pipe, c. 1850

Germany (expressionist, 1920–1930): George Grosz, *Untitled,* c. 1930

America (early 20th century): Walking Couple, c. 1980

Europe (surrealist, 1930s): Hans Bellmer, *La Poupée,* 1936

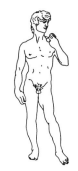

America (prehistoric: Native American, Mimbres, Southwest, 1000 B.C.–A.D. 1492): Ceramic Pottery, A.D. 500

Europe (medieval, A.D. 300–1450): *The Golden Age (manuscript illumination),* 4th century A.D.

China, (from A.D. 100): *Early Illustrated Love Manuals,* A.D. 618–907

India (Hindu, A.D. 650–1750): *Temple Sculpture,* A.D. 900–1300

Italy (renaissance, 1250–1550): Michelangelo Buonarroti, *David,* 1501–1504

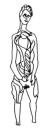

9

France (rococo, early 18th century): Jean-Honoré Fragonard, *The Happy Lovers,* c. 1767

America (colonial, 1650–1776): Female Figure, 18th century

Solomon Islands (19th–20th centuries): *Hunter,* 19th–20th centuries

Ghana, western Africa (Ashanti, 19th century): *Brass Gold-weight,* c. 1850

France (19th century): Gustave Courbet, *The Origin of the World,* 1866

France (1950s): Jean Dubuffet, *Couple,* 1950

America (1970s–1990s): Mose Tolliver, Lady on a Scooter, c. 1970

America (1960s): Tom Wesselmann, Great American Nude, 1967

Europe (1960s): Pablo Picasso, *Untitled,* 1968

America (1980s–1990s): Jeff Koons, Jeff on Top (Dirty), 1991

From religious celebrations of sexuality in the prehistoric pueblo, to clandestine expressions in puritanical New England, American erotica has always been diverse.

The first section of this book presents some of the earliest examples of erotic art in America. Representing a vast period of time—from the first until the eighteenth centuries A.D.—these images and objects bear witness to the **cultural diversity** that continues to define the American experience. From the petroglyphs and decorated pottery of the prehistoric pueblo in the Southwest, to funerary ceramics of the Southeast, to beautifully carved weapons from the Northeast, and finally to utilitarian objects from the Northwest Coast region of this country, the varying **cultural significance of sexuality** in Native American life becomes evident in the different ways that indigenous artists sought to express it. Likewise, erotica dating back to colonial America provides a **glimpse into social views**—and deviations thereof—about **sex during this formative period of the nation's history.**

It would be a mistake to consider these earliest examples of American erotic art as unusual or isolated phenomena—indeed, they have a place in the global context of world art, throughout which one finds a flowering of erotic expression. In the pre-Columbian world of South America, artists of the Moche society (600–200 B.C.) and later of the Chimu people (A.D. 1000–1470) fashioned ceramic pots representing a range of **sexual activities.** Far Eastern cultures have produced a wealth of erotica—in China, illustrated Taoist love manuals guided couples through the vicissitudes of lovemaking, while in Japan, the genre of printed images known as Shunga provided viewers with a forbidden view of the demimonde. In India, Hindu temples were adorned with sculptural tableaux representing divine acts of copulation, and the Hindu sex manual known as the *Kamasutra* is by now a world-famous lexicon of exotic erotica. In the Oceanic world, **sexually explicit** carvings were produced for the religious purpose of ensuring fertility, and throughout Africa, exquisite objects and images, from Madagascar to the Ivory Coast, represent a range of **sexual practices** centered in a variety of cultural contexts. From the sacred to the profane, and from the practical to the purely aesthetic, erotic artworks from this vast and diverse history provide a fascinating visual record of human sexuality, to which America's artists have made significant contributions.

In the pueblo region of the southwestern United States, highly stylized figural petroglyphs—rock drawings made by cutting away at the surface—have survived as a somewhat **cryptic visual record** of the daily activities and religious beliefs of prehistoric Native Americans. Several examples of such drawings existing in Utah contain unmistakably **erotic imagery,** characterized on the one hand by the figures' enlarged genitalia, both male and female, and on the other hand by the dramatic depiction of **sexual intercourse.** It is believed that such scenes were created within a religious context and perhaps relate to sacred rituals conducted in order to ensure fertility. The fact that these images of copulation and dancing are not isolated, but generally appear with other symbolic images, suggests that they represent what was part of a holistic world view.

A very different tradition of artmaking survives in adorned ceramic bowls made by the Mimbres people (c. A.D. 500). Embellished with figurative imagery that balances graceful geometric stylization with a surprising degree of naturalism, these coil-made vessels are marked by a mix of exquisite decoration and practical narrative. Bearing vivid scenes both religious and secular—the two were inextricably linked—they provide us with a rare and intimate glimpse into the lives of the early inhabitants of New Mexico. Some of these scenes are erotic, offering explicit views of anatomy and sexual intercourse, but as in

12

the case of the above-mentioned tradition of petroglyphs, there is every indication that such graphic scenes belonged within the comprehensive context of Mimbres beliefs and lifeways. That these bowls were recovered at ancient burial sites, each bowl marked with a hole that scholars believe to indicate a ceremonial "killing," is further proof that the **eroticism** one finds depicted in their decoration was an integral part of **Mimbres spirituality.** Aesthetically very different, voluptuous ceramic objects associated with mortuary sites of the American Southeast nevertheless reveal a similarly holistic world view held by the Mississippian culture (c.1200–1700). These objects testify to their makers' belief in the connection between this life and the next, and the important role of sexuality in both spheres. Very different are the **pleasurable,** and even **whimsical,** examples of erotica found in the Northeast, and on the Northwest Coast, which reveal an impulse to alleviate the burden posed by otherwise quotidian activities. In all, the indigenous American art historical record from this period of time reveals richly diverse manifestations of the erotic.

The sparse examples of erotic art produced by European settlers in colonial America belong in a general sense to the context of world art, but more specifically, they hark to the visual tradition of Western art. From the fecund fertility goddesses of the Paleolithic to the idealized statuary of classical Greece, depictions of the figure in Western art have consistently been charged, to varying degrees, with eroticism. From the Renaissance period of Michelangelo and Giulio Romano, to the Baroque era of Bernini, and from the Rococo caprices of Antoine Watteau and Jean-Honoré Fragonard, to the whimsical scenes of Thomas Rowlandson and the outrageous fin-de-siècle fantasies of John Beardsley, the history of "high" art in the West survives as **a celebration of sexuality,** even as subsequent populist image-making traditions, made possible with the advent of printmaking, have given

us more accessible and increasingly bawdy examples of erotica, such as French eighteenth-century engraved illustrations of the popular British novel *Fanny Hill.*

But life in colonial America was, to be sure, not so typically libertine as the London of Hogarth or the Paris of Boucher. By dramatic contrast to the comparatively freer Native American views about sexuality, which the colonists with their puritanical beliefs abhorred as immoral, sex was limited to the institution of marriage, and **deviations** such as **extramarital** or **homosexual relations** bore harsh penalties indeed.

The few examples of erotica that survive from this period reflect these restrictive mores. Nude representations of men from this period are virtually nonexistent, and there is a near-palpable ambivalence evident in existing sexual depictions of women, which betrays a **sense of guilt for indulging in forbidden fruit.** Exquisitely incised powder horns dating from the French and Indian War of the mid-eighteenth century reflect the relatively repressed nature of sexual expression in colonial New England. Curator and author Robert F. Trent has traced the visual sources of the horns' imagery to a range of traditions both "high" and "low," arguing that the unstable psychology of the soldiers, cut off as they were from family and female companionship, gave rise to unusual artistic expressions. Yet the erotic content found in this genre was typically subdued, emerging only in veiled symbolism or in clever examples of textual play. Such restraint in **American visual erotica,** however, would alter dramatically in subsequent centuries, as artists kept apace with rapid changes in societal views of sexuality.

NATIVE AMERICAN
(FREMONT)
Utah
Petroglyphs
A.D. 1–1000

Nine Mile Canyon, Utah
Petroglyphs
A.D. 950–1200

(opposite) Photographer Leon C. Yost, a specialist in the field of petroglyphs, has captured several vivid examples of prehistoric Native American erotica. Depicting a couple about to engage in coitus, the artist of this rock drawing has rendered the central male and female figures in a schematic fashion, with the emphasis on their highly exaggerated genitals. The action is focused on the act of intercourse to the exclusion of all else—the man lunges, his oversize penis erect, less toward the woman than toward her swollen, larger-than-life vagina itself. Such images were not considered lewd, but rather a natural expression of sexuality, albeit within the all-important context of ensuring fertility and the survival of the people.
(right) This rock drawing narrates important ritual aspects of ancient fertility beliefs. Three men, gracefully rendered as abstracted stick figures, each brandish a large "planting stick," as well as an erect penis. Such sticks were often placed in the ground as part of a prayer for fertility, while the erect penises symbolize both procreation and the power of hunters. According to legend, the hump appearing on each figure's back indicates a load of gifts for young ladies, seeds, or perhaps babies.
(on page 10) Ute petroglyphs of male and female sexual activity, ca. 1600–1900. The vulva areas of the two female figures show evidence of rubbing. It is thought that this may be the result of repeated visits to this site by woman who wished to gain the power of fertility contained here.

16

NATIVE AMERICAN
(MIMBRES)
New Mexico
• *Ceramic Bowl*
c. A.D. 700–1100
between 7–10″
Collection of Bradley Smith

• *Ceramic Bowl*
c. A.D. 700–1100
between 7–10″
Collection of Bradley Smith

• *Ceramic Bowl*
c. A.D. 500
3 1/2 × 7 3/8″
Collection of Stéphane Janssen

• *Ceramic Bowl* *(opposite)*
c. A.D. 700–1100
between 7–10″
Collection of Bradley Smith

(top left) This scenario, which recounts hunting exploits of an unusual sort, adds a certain depth to the notion of the prehistoric pueblo inhabitants' sense of unity with nature. Two men are shown engaged in the sexual conquest of a wild animal—as one attempts to control the beast from the front, the other engages in rear penetration. A high degree of decorative artistry transforms this act of bestial buggery into a whimsical and entertaining tableau.

(center left) Depicting a hunter sporting his catch of the day as well as a sizable erection, this artist has cleverly equated the hunter's prowess and his virility.

Naturalistic detail in the rendering of both man and rabbit is counterbalanced by an abstract checkerboard pattern and the artist's graceful economy of line to create a lively composition.

(bottom left) Evidence that homosexuality was but one of a variety of sexual practices within Mimbres culture, this scene is a curious one. Depicting what appears to be a sneak attack, one man penetrates another, the latter apparently his rather unwilling quarry. But the atmosphere of this graceful image is less violent than it is subtly humorous.

(opposite) This image depicts what is likely an early example of sex education, conducted within a ceremonial setting. A male of some stature, possibly a shaman, vigorously demonstrates the vicissitudes of sexual intercourse for a captive audience. The artist's decision to provide an X-ray anatomical view of the participants was not inspired by a prurient impulse, but rather a practical, didactic one.

18

NATIVE AMERICAN
(MISSISSIPPIAN)
New Madrid, Missouri
• *Ceramic Effigy Bottle*
A.D. 1200–1400
6 1/8″ high
Museum für Völkerkunde,
Vienna, Austria

This rather crude female figure exemplifies the stylistic repertoire of Mississippian effigy pottery. Animal forms such as frogs and owls were also popular. Anatomical approximation, rather than realism, was the artist's modus operandi in creating an object that served to memorialize the deceased. Despite its unrefined look, this figure's exaggerated proportions bear a surprisingly voluptuous charm. The full, round breasts are punctuated with erect, well-articulated nipples, and the heavy lower body swells to fertility goddess proportions. This bottle's subtle eroticism belies its funereal function.

NATIVE AMERICAN
(MISSISSIPPIAN)
Southeast
Ceramic Frog Teapot
c. A.D. 1400–1600
9 1/2" high
Collection of Linda and
Gene Kangas

The teapot form was introduced
to the artisans of the Mississippian culture by the early explor-
ers of the American Southeast.
Here is a bawdy variation on
that often-mundane theme. A
bloated frog comprises the body
of this pot, out of whose mouth
protrudes an unmistakably phallic form, which serves as a
spout. While one might choose
to see this simply as a frog in the
act of capturing his prey with a
sticky tongue, the suggestion of
fellatio cannot be ignored.

NATIVE AMERICAN
(MISSISSIPPIAN)
Southeast
Ceramic Breast Pot
c. A.D. 700–1700
8 1/2" high
Collection of Linda and
Gene Kangas

Form follows function in the
case of this cleverly realized
water bottle. Made in the shape
of a fecund, milk-laden breast,
this vessel is equal parts utilitarian object and visual pun. The
full form of the breast combines
contrasting notions of maternal
nurture and erotic pleasure.

ARTIST UNKNOWN
Sandwich, Massachusetts
Female Figure
18th century
chestnut wood
16 × 4 × 2″
Marvill Collection

Staring into space with bright
blue pewter eyes, this
grotesque figure brings to mind
the stereotypical witch. Here,
evil is equated with sexual
promiscuity—this American
Medusa lewdly holds up her
skirt for all to see, leaving
exposed her vividly detailed
vagina. She likely stood as a
warning to good women of the
dangers of desire.

NATIVE AMERICAN
(PROBABLY EASTERN WOODLANDS)
New Sweden on
the Delaware River
● *Wooden Ball-Headed Club*
c. 1650
wood with inlays of white shell
and copper
24″ long
Skoklosters Slott,
Bälstad, Sweden

This wooden club, richly inlaid
with white wampum shell and
copper decoration, was likely
collected around 1650 in the
colony of New Sweden on the
Delaware River. Thought to
have functioned in a ceremonial
context, this exquisite weapon
is a fantastical hybrid of human
and animal forms. The ball, or
striking end of the club, has
been carved into a head with a
grotesque face, which in turn
appears to be caught in the
maw of a ferocious lizard. Yet
the fierceness of the imagery on
the club's top half stands in
marked contrast to its lower
portion, which tapers into a
very sensuous handle in the
shape of a feminine leg. The
owner would have grasped an
invitingly articulated calf, a tender and erotic contrast to this
object's inherent power.

NATIVE AMERICAN
Northwest Coast
● *Hand Hammer*
18th century
stone
8 1/4 × 3 1/2 × 2 3/4″
American Primitive Gallery,
New York

Derived from ancient phallic
stone pestles, which were used
to grind foodstuffs in vaginal-
shaped mortars, handheld hammers such as this one evolved
into general-use tools. Although
overtly penis-shaped examples
exist, most often such hammers
are nonspecifically phallic, as
in the case of this particular
one, which is marked by a
nipple-shaped top. The
metaphorical potential of this
shape is fulfilled when put into
use—gripped tightly during the
course of repeated pounding,
the sexual double entendre
becomes obvious.

ATTRIBUTED TO RICHARDSON
MINOR (LAKE GEORGE SCHOOL)
(1736–1797)
Crown Point, New York
Stephen Tambling Horn
1761
horn, pine, iron,
and black pigment
5 1/2″ long
Collection of James E. Routh, Jr.

Incised horns such as this one
were used by soldiers to carry
gunpowder for their muskets.

The images and inscriptions
that adorn powder horns often
reflect the loneliness and sexual
restlessness experienced by the
young soldiers, deprived as
they were of the comforts of
both home and companionship.
This horn was owned by one
Stephen Tambling (b. 1738), a
native of Windham, Connecticut, and a soldier in the Fourth
Connecticut Regiment in 1758,
during the French and Indian
War. Incised with decorative
motifs as well as text by the
artist Richardson Minor (whose

signature is visible on one
side), the horn's inscription
reads as follows: Curteous lady
these lines I do present/Unto
You to give your Heart
Content/Not only this but will-
ing would kneel/The first letter
of Each line to feel. The first
letter of each line, when read
on the horn in a column from
top to bottom, together spell
the word *cunt. (A detail of
this inscription is provided on
page 11.)*

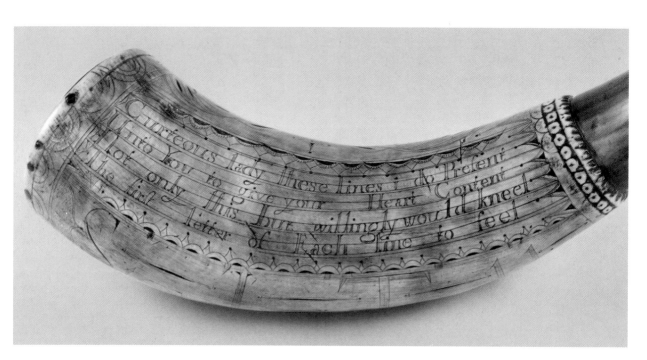

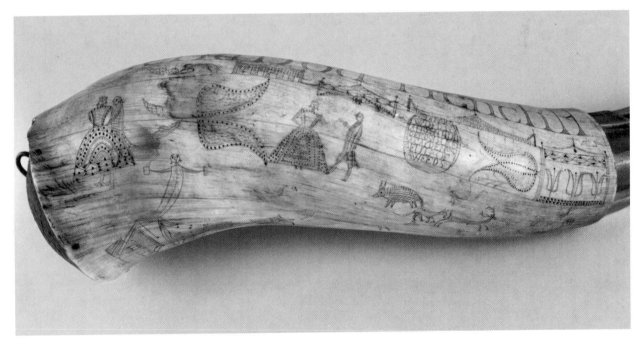

ARTIST UNKNOWN
(LAKE GEORGE SCHOOL)
Lake George, New York
Sergeant Ichabod French Horn
c. 1755–1757
horn, pine, and iron
19 1/2″ long
Collection of
William H. Guthman

This powder horn was owned
by a Sergeant Ichabod French
(1730–1763) of Guilford,
Connecticut, a soldier who
served as a private, a ranger,
and a sergeant in various mili-
tary campaigns of the French
and Indian War between 1755
and 1758. On one side, the
owner's name has been incised,
and the other side bears decorative motifs that include a
tulip, a two-masted ship with
an accompanying mermaid,
and a couple executing different dance steps. It is thought
that the mermaid and the
dancing couple bespeak the
soldier's fear of possible
spousal infidelity.

PART 2

Love
1850

Despite the Victorian restrictions that marked nineteenth-century American society, a freer sexuality became evident in a range of nonacademic artmaking practices.

The sweeping changes that were to alter the social fabric of America in the course of the nineteenth century had, as might be expected, a significant impact on American sexuality and collectively held views about gender identity. With the rise of industrialization and urbanization, the earlier **puritanical controls on sexual practices,** enforced by both church and state, gradually weakened, resulting in a generally freer sexual atmosphere. The family remained the all-important social unit, but sex was no longer so strictly limited to within its confines—especially in the case of men. The emergence of a powerful middle class was accompanied by a new concern for **imposing limits on childbearing,** particularly in the service of facilitating financial gain. In their book *Intimate Matters: A History of Sexuality in America* (1988), authors John D'Emilio and Estelle B. Freedman have argued that these new controls over reproduction succeeded, first, in weakening the link between sex and childbearing, and, second, in linking sexuality to intimacy and love. What resulted was a greater exploration of the **pleasures of erotic life,** not only within the marriage but also in a variety of **extramarital sexual pursuits— prostitution, premarital sex, homosexuality,** and even the utopian ideology of free love were all on the rise. Modern life and, with it, modern sexuality, consistently reflected in the folk and popular arts, had emerged by century's end.

But these changes came gradually. The ideals of British Victorian society infused American life; the **Victorian notion of pure and noble womanhood** proved nearly as limiting to the lives of American women as earlier Puritan morality had. Society's views of women came to be split, therefore, between the ideal of the chaste wife, untainted by the moral burden of lust, and the spectre of the whore, morally bankrupt in her sexual promiscuity. Nowhere is this pervasive virgin/whore dichotomy more evident than in the arts made by and for men whose occupations separated them from their female counterparts, specifically sailors and whalers.

Commerce on the sea—shipping as well as hunting whales for valuable oil—thrived during the nineteenth century, and with it art forms such as ships' figureheads and scrimshaw flourished. The ancient tradition of figureheads took on particularly American significance in a plethora of full- and three-quarter-length protectresses, carved to adorn the prows of sailing ships. Influenced by the sculptural vocabulary of the classical revival, artists fashioned noble beauties embodying the **Victorian ideal of purity** who were charged with both protecting the ships and reminding the seamen of **faithful wives and lovers** back home.

The term *scrimshaw*, which refers to the practice of engraving whale ivory and baleen, is thought by some to have evolved from the words *scrim* (to scrimp or economize) and *shaw* (to saw) or *shand* (to sand). Scrimshanders were generally sailors on whaling boats who plied their art both to kill time and to make gifts for loved ones they had left behind. Although most surviving examples of scrimshaw attest to the makers' respect for the morally ideal woman, a few works reveal a very different, even **pornographic, impulse** envisioning women of a **morally looser, sexually experienced** sort. The majority of works that fall into the latter category were cast out to sea by guilty sailors in acts of censorial penance, often at the behest of their ships' captains, before returning to port and the strictures of society that awaited. Yet **chaste or lurid,** these scrimshanded representations of the opposite sex are all infused with some **level of eroticism.**

Native American peoples in the nineteenth century continued to be characterized as sexually freer than their neighbors of European descent, a fact that fueled the clash between cultures. Carved and adorned objects from different regions survive as a record of the consistently less constricted sexual mores of indigenous people. Named for the artist George Catlin, who spent a good deal of time recording the lifeways of Plains Indians, pipe bowls carved out of red steatite (later named catlinite) indicate a variety of sex practices, including **homosexuality,** anal coitus, as well as a healthy sense of **sexual humor.** Another genre in which sexual imagery flourished was the ritual effigy stick. Overall, these art-making traditions provide a counterpoint to the more gradual emergence of non–Native American erotica.

The slow but steady increase of **sexual awareness** and activities in nineteenth-century America was especially evidenced in the rapidly emerging genre of erotic toys, or novelties, that remains popular today. Often portable, such objects were usually kept hidden from view themselves or involved some type of concealment in their construction. Popular in this genre is the **"peekaboo"** piece, in which a benign "before" view gives way to a sexually explicit "after" view. Such hidden erotica is unmistakably charged with a **sense of voyeurism** and serves as a reminder that the need to hide remained, despite a considerably freer atmosphere. Many of these movable novelties typically involve some kind of humor in their actions. The kinds of humor chosen by various artists to extract a blush or a knowing chuckle from novelty viewers/users are varied indeed, ranging from the straightforward shock of suddenly revealed anatomy, to more subversive transgressions of accepted sexual norms to reduce—for a moment at least—the **sexual act** to a comic event.

Utilitarian and sporting objects made by and for men comprise a significant percentage of nineteenth-century erotic folk art and Americana from this period, a fact that is betrayed by a noticeable focus on the female nude.

Folk canes, used not merely to lean on but rather to establish one's identity in the face of one's peers, were often decorated with figurative, **sexually explicit forms.** Workmen's tools and gear, another bastion of masculinity, were yet another sphere in which decorative erotica flourished. Adorned with sexually oriented images, these objects were truly transformed, and the workday significantly enlivened. From sensuously carved fishing rods to richly embellished hunting rifles, sportsmen asserted their social territory with images that would have been considered unacceptable in mixed company. In all, different artists' visions of the erotic added a certain **clandestine spice to the activities**—both work and play—enjoyed by men.

Although largely the province of men, erotica produced during the nineteenth century slowly filtered into other aspects of daily life, shared by men and women alike. From kitchen tools to exercise aids, a varied erotic vocabulary entered American life to an unprecedented degree, foreshadowing the revolutions in sexual awareness that would come to define the subsequent century.

The late nineteenth century was marked by the onset of a variety of social movements that involved the emergence of women from domestic life into public life. Concurrently, reactions against **sexual promiscuity** and other activities deemed immoral were attempts to stem the tide of cultural developments that were by now integral elements of American life. But these movements were part of the **larger push for women's equality.** By the end of the century, women were a force to be reckoned within American society, and this hard-won power was reflected in contemporary, fashionable, albeit ever **eroticized, images of women.** This fin-de-siècle shift in mood toward the distinctly modern in visual folk and pop-cultural erotica provides but a glimpse of what was yet to come.

ARTIST UNKNOWN
New York State
● *Three Gallon Ovoid "Slave Jug"*
c. 1810–1815
incised, cobalt blue decorated
salt-glaze stoneware
17″ high
America Hurrah Antiques,
New York

Here, a traditional ceramic
ovoid form has been brought
to life with a playfully erotic
image. The only decoration
adorning this plain but elegant
jug is the image of a woman
who confronts the viewer
with more than just her face.
Upside down, she peers
through her open legs, but it is
her ample derriere that takes
top billing in this intimate performance.

ARTIST UNKNOWN
● *Phallic Bottle*
c. 1840
brown glassware
$9\,1/2 \times 6\,1/2 \times 4\,1/8″$
The Kinsey Institute for
Research in Sex, Gender and
Reproduction,
Bloomington, Indiana

Two separate pieces of glass
were blown to create this bottle. The lower part swells into
two bulbous areas, from which
the neck emerges in a vertical
line, creating the effect of an
erect penis with two testicles.
The charm of this very unique
object lies in its sly understate-
ment. In refraining from the
impulse to add graphic detail,
the artist has effectively sug-
gested the male organ without
compromising the bottle's
abstract beauty.

Toby Pitchers
c. 1810
ceramic, color glazes, yellow
earthenware, Rockingham glaze
(front) 10 1/2 × 5 × 9″
(back) 9 × 4 1/2 × 7 1/2″
The Kinsey Institute for
Research in Sex, Gender and
Reproduction,
Bloomington, Indiana

The colorful pitcher featured in
the foreground is a bawdy variation of the typical toby jug, a
genre of ceramics that scholars
trace to late-eighteenth-century
England. The character is based
on a fictional toper named Toby
Eillpot, whose drinking exploits
were recounted in the famous
song "The Brown Jug," first published in 1761. Although the
typical toby jug presents the old
fellow seated, wearing a tri-
cornered hat and clutching his
ale mug, the American version
is an impious double entendre—the spout is also Toby's
erect penis—which is thought
to be a colonial spoof on the
British. In the background
stands a similar pitcher finished
in a rich brown Rockingham
glaze, which complements
Toby's impressive silhouette.
Whether Toby's good humor is
due to the spirits he has
imbibed or to his state of
arousal—or to both—is for the
viewer to decide.

ARTIST UNKNOWN
Newburyport, Massachusetts
• *Carved Female Figure*
c. 1850
ivory
2 1/2″ high
Collection of Brian and
Nancy Cullity

This small, carved figure probably served as a toothpick.
Fashioned either by a prisoner
of war, a sailor, or a whaler, this
rather awkward actualization of
the female body was perhaps an
important daily reminder, to its
itinerant owner, of a faraway
sweetheart. The artist has created the likeness of a buxom
woman who seductively holds
her dress up in order to reveal
herself. This piece takes on an
intimate, even sensual, quality
if one considers its everyday
contact with the unknown
user's mouth.

ARTIST UNKNOWN
Massachusetts
• *Pie Crimper*
c. 1850
whale ivory
8 1/2 × 4 × 1 1/4″
Collection of Steve Miller

Carved from whalebone, this
exquisitely modeled nude
doubles as artwork and tool.
A flattened handle takes the
place of the figure's head,
and between her feet, the
spokes of the crimping mechanism turn like a unicycle wheel
when in use. A forked attach-
ment in front appears to be an
unmistakably phallic penetration of her sex.

ARTIST UNKNOWN
Pennsylvania
• *Book Sculpture*
c. 1840
polychromed wood, wire,
and metal
8 × 10 3/8 × 2 5/8″ (closed)
Collection of Dr. and
Mrs. Bruce E. Ettinger

This elegant book cover does
not contain printed pages but
instead conceals a fantastical
sculptural group that pops into
view at its owner's bidding.
This orgy scene is like no other.
A dog, with its tongue hanging
out, supports two frenetically
copulating couples; set in
motion, the group forms a
dynamic and exciting totality.

NATIVE AMERICAN
(SIOUX)
Wahpeton, North Dakota
• *Pipe Bowl*
c. 1880–1910
catlinite
7 3/4″ high
National Museum of the
American Indian, Smithsonian
Institution, New York

(top) This pipe bowl, which
would have been attached to a
long stem when in use, reveals
its Sioux maker's good sense of
humor and clever use of the
basic pipe bowl shape. The end
of the shank, or horizontal element, has been transformed into
a witty caricature of a white
man. He is rendered with pinched features and characteristic
hat, lying prone. The bowl itself
emerges from between his legs
to suggest a grotesquely enlarged penis, from which, one must
imagine, smoke would rise
when in use. The pipe is also
embellished with effigy images
of a buffalo head and a turtle.

32

NATIVE AMERICAN
(PROBABLY PAWNEE)
• *Pipe Bowl*
mid-19th century
catlinite and blackstone
5 3/8″: man 2 3/8″
National Museum of the
American Indian, Smithsonian
Institution, New York

(center) Comprised of two separate parts—a catlinite bowl and
shank, and a pair of blackstone
figures—this pipe bowl unit is
both charming and exquisite.
The carved couple provides a
pleasing formal counterpoint to
the adjacent circular bowl. Both
male and female face the same
direction, she in front and he
behind with arms outstretched
to hold her in place. By rendering the figures with knees bent,
and with only the slightest point
of contact between them, the
artist has subtly conveyed the
act of anal intercourse.

NATIVE AMERICAN
(DAKOTA)
Western Great Lakes,
Eastern Dakotas
• *Pipe Bowl*
mid-19th century
catlinite
6 1/4″ long
Berne Historical Museum
of Ethnography,
Berne, Switzerland

(bottom) The homoerotic over-
tones of this rare and elegantly
carved pipe bowl are unmistakable. Wrapped around the end
of the shank, the supple, nude
figure of a youth plainly suggests sexual availability. His
buttocks open to form the
bowl itself.

NATIVE AMERICAN
(WOODLANDS)
Minnesota
• *Pipe Bowl*
c. 1880
wood
2 × 1 × 1 3/4″
Collection of Steve Miller

(opposite) The beauty of this
pipe bowl lies in its simplicity.
Consisting of the carved figure
of a headless and squatting
woman, the way in which the
artist has linked form and function draws out its crude eroticism. The approximated torso is
punctuated with two stylized
breasts, above which gapes the
bowl's opening. The hole
between this eerily anonymous
figure's legs invites the user to
insert and eventually draw from
the pipe's stem.

ARTIST UNKNOWN
Sacramento, California
Couple on a Table
1850–1852
cast replica of original bronze
2 3/4 × 3″
The Kinsey Institute for
Research in Sex, Gender
and Reproduction,
Bloomington, Indiana

This bas-relief plaque takes us
beyond the missionary position
to an intimate scene of domestic gymnastics. A woman leans
back on a table, hooking one
leg over the shoulder of her
standing partner. This work is a
cast replica of an earlier bronze
piece that was retrieved in an
excavation of old Sacramento.
It is likely that such plaques
adorned the walls of bordellos
for the edification of patrons.

ARTIST UNKNOWN
New England
Portrait Bust
1835
polychromed wood
9 1/2 × 6 × 41 1/4″
Private Collection

While American portrait busts
of the nineteenth century were
often inspired by the classical
revival—romantic visions of
idealized heroines in billowing
robes—this example is more
realistic, down to earth, and
frankly erotic. Painted to give
the impression of warm, ample
flesh and familiar features, this
figure may have been created
with a specific lady in mind.

ARTIST UNKNOWN
San Francisco
Scrimshaw
1880–1890
Polychromed scrimshawed
walrus tusk
18 × 3″
Collection of
A.J. DeFalco, D.D.S.

That this example of overtly erotic scrimshaw has survived to be photographed intact is nothing short of a miracle. Such pieces are extremely rare, as it was common practice on whaling ships that handworked erotica be destroyed before returning to port, at the insistence of a sailor's captain or the seaman's own conscience. Front and back views reveal incised and colored sexual fantasies that may have been inspired by a visit to a bordello—scenes of sexual intercourse are mixed with other generous views of feminine anatomy. A detail *(opposite)* features one intimate scenario, in which a man uses his fingers to stimulate his lover. The style is typically naive and perhaps derives from sources in popular illustration.

ARTIST UNKNOWN
Love 1850
1850
scrimshaw
5 1/2 × 2 1/8 × 1 3/8″
Private Collection

The practice of incising ivory and baleen from whales was a popular pastime for lonely whalers. The sperm whale provided teeth such as this one on which a scrimshander could bring to life images of wives or lovers back home. This scene, although relatively tender, is shot through with a subdued eroticism—in the center, a gentleman embraces his sweetheart, while an excited voyeur looks on. *(See page 25 for a detail in color.)*

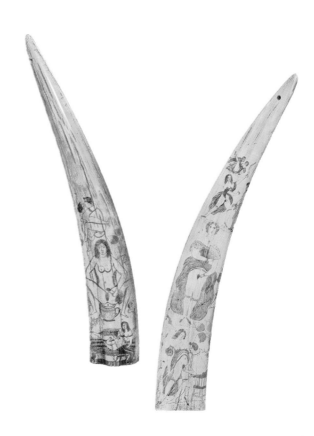

ARTIST UNKNOWN
Michigan
Carpenter's Tool Chest Lid
(detail)
late 19th century
painted wood
approximately 15″ high
Collection of Louis and
Colleen Picek

(opposite) Although somewhat
crude, this artist's depiction of a
nude on the lid of a tool chest
suggests voluptuousness with a
few well-placed lines. Posing
suggestively atop a barrel, and
wearing nothing but shoes, she
doubtless enlivened the otherwise mundane workday of Joe
L. Hale, the carpenter who used
this tool chest.

ARTIST UNKNOWN
Found in Indiana
Coffin
1875–1880
walnut with wire latch
$7/8 \times 1 1/4 \times 4 1/2$″
Collection of Susan Parrett
and Rod Lich

(top right) Novelty items such as
this one, in which a facade may
be removed to reveal a naughty
view, were popular during this
period. Closed, it is simply a
miniature coffin, but once
opened, the alleged corpse
springs to life.

ATTRIBUTED TO HENRY CLAY NYE
Sandwich, Massachusetts
Carved Vulva
19th century
wood
20″ overall length
Collection of
Brian and Nancy Cullity

(bottom right) Carved in rich
detail, this image of a vulva is
rare indeed. Larger than life and
disembodied, this object bears
an uncannily erotic appeal, providing as it does an unusually
thorough view of that element
of female anatomy most often
shrouded in mystery.

ARTIST UNKNOWN
New England
Nude Woman Cane
1880
painted wood
shaft length–36″
Collection of Steve Miller

(opposite) Carved canes were, and still are, both utilitarian objects and a means of expressing one's individuality. Largely the province of men, canes such as this one represented the female body for the purpose of providing erotic titillation. Positioned upside down and with legs invitingly spread apart, this fleshy figure offered a handful for whomever used this cane.

ARTIST UNKNOWN
Penis Cane
1890–1910
wood
35 × 5¼″
Collection of
Herbert Waide Hemphill, Jr.

Featuring a carved penis for a handle, this cane may have once been used by a woman. Offering an exquisitely simple but potent visual pun, this clever cane places its user both literally and figuratively in control.

ARTIST UNKNOWN
Articulated Figure
1880
polychromed wood
10 3/8 × 1 3/4 × 1 1/4"
Collection of Kirk Landauer

An example of the popular
genre of concealed erotica,
this distinguished gentleman,
thought to be a crude represen-
tation of Abraham Lincoln, cuts
a very different figure "after"
than "before." This whimsical
figure's limbs aren't the only
articulated elements. Upon
removing a small front section,
the sixteenth president is
revealed to be sporting a
sizable erection.

42

ARTIST UNKNOWN
Ohio
Saint Peter
c. 1850
glazed ceramic
6 × 1 1/2"
Collection of Susan Parrett
and Rod Lich

The genre of sewer tile art—
sculpture made by sewer tile
factory laborers in their spare
time—inspired this classic sexual double entendre. Here, the
sacred has been mixed together
with the profane—Saint Peter,
traditionally known as the pillar
of the Catholic Church, has
been transformed into a pillar
of a different sort. Sculpted on
one side of the tile is the venerable saint himself, appearing in
a tunic, with hands clasped,
and his signature beard. But the
other side is a different story
altogether: Saint Peter's back
becomes a life-size replica of an
erect penis. This visual pun also
evokes a common linguistic
one—a common slang word for
penis is *peter*. This hand-
fashioned image has become so
popular over the years that it
has been replicated and mass-
produced in molded ceramic.

ARTIST UNKNOWN
Found in Michigan
● *Yankee Salute*
1860
tin
3 × 1 1/2″ extended
Collection of Susan Parrett
and Rod Lich

The humor that is always evident in sexual novelties such as
this takes on a greater significance when the allegiances of
its maker are considered. The
Confederate soldier who fashioned this toy likely intended
it as an insult to his Yankee
enemies. When the figure is
manipulated into a salute, more
than just its chubby arm snaps
to attention.

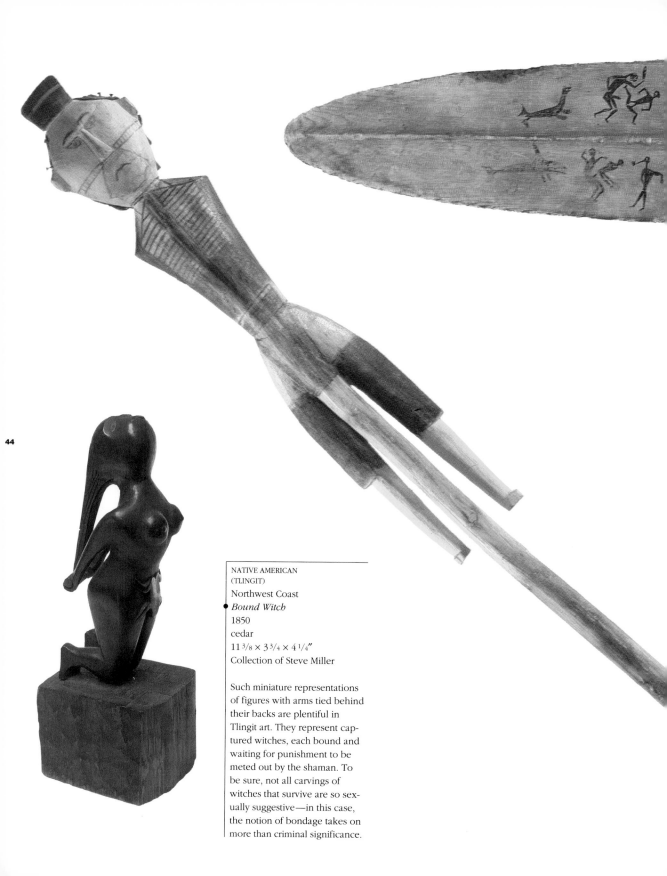

NATIVE AMERICAN
(TLINGIT)
Northwest Coast
● *Bound Witch*
1850
cedar
11 3/8 × 3 3/4 × 4 1/4″
Collection of Steve Miller

Such miniature representations
of figures with arms tied behind
their backs are plentiful in
Tlingit art. They represent captured witches, each bound and
waiting for punishment to be
meted out by the shaman. To
be sure, not all carvings of
witches that survive are so sexually suggestive—in this case,
the notion of bondage takes on
more than criminal significance.

NATIVE AMERICAN
(ESKIMO)
Southwest Alaska
● *Incised Paddle*
19th century
wood
57 1/2″ long
The British Museum,
London, England

While three-dimensional erotica is quite rare in Eskimo art, a healthy attitude toward sexuality is evident in incised imagery, such as the mythical orgy scene that embellishes this paddle. Scratched into the wood and then filled in with either soot or grease, the human and animal figures that animate this orgy scene are both delicate and lively. Interspersed between scenes of hunting and everyday life appear couples and intimate groups, both in boats and on land, engaged in various sexual acts. It is thought that these images were intended to promote animal fertility.

NATIVE AMERICAN
(TETON SIOUX)
● *Human Effigy*
Victory Dance Stick
1876–1887
painted wood
24 1/2″ long
Smithsonian Institution,
Washington, D.C.

A caricature of grand proportions, this Teton Sioux human effigy stick was made to poke fun at, and humiliate, enemies. Complete with dour expression and missing its arms, this figure's legs are dwarfed by its gigantic phallus, which would have been symbolically manipulated by the stick's user, adding insult to injury.

ARTIST UNKNOWN
Northeast
● *Tobacco Cleaver*
c. 1880
steel, brass, and bone
$8\,3/4 \times 3\,3/4''$
Collection of Jonathan Holstein

This diminutive tool is also a
subtly erotic artwork. Used to
chop tobacco leaves, the handle
of this tool has been shaped to
get the job done, but also to
please the eye and the hand.
Form and function become
one—a curvaceous woman
appears to be engaged in calis-
thenics, an action that complements the chopping motion
effected by this tool's user.

ARTIST UNKNOWN
● *Snuffbox*
c. 1880
wood
$2 \times 1/2 \times 3\,1/2''$
Private Collection

According to Sigmund Freud,
one of the sexual fetishist's
favorite objects of lust is the
woman's shoe. Although it is
unlikely that the maker of this
clever snuffbox had psychoana-
lytic theory in mind, the artist's
equation of a lady's shoe with
overtly phallic eroticism is no
mere coincidence. The lid of the
box consists of a man's figure
punctuated by an erection. To
slide the lid open and thereby
gain access to the snuff within,
one must remove the penis.

ARTIST UNKNOWN
Pennsylvania
● *Calipers*
c. 1890
tin
7″ high
American Primitive Gallery,
New York

A simple measuring tool has here
become the springboard for an
artist's formal wit. Consisting of
male and female nude silhou-
ettes fastened at the top, these
calipers take on new, erotic significance when opened and closed for the purpose of measuring.

ARTIST UNKNOWN
Found in Buck's County,
Pennsylvania
Artist and Model
c. 1880–1890
oil on linen canvas
24 × 20"
Private Collection

This painting is a charming
addition to the once-popular
genre dedicated to depicting
the artist busy at work in the
studio with his model. For its
time, this scene is rather
risqué—conspicuously absent
is the requisite matronly chaper-
one, usually present to prevent
any extracurricular activities.
The result is an erotically
charged atmosphere. A rich,
Victorian setting echoes the
voluptuousness of the model's
body, posed to suggestively
reveal as much as possible,
especially her substantial backside. This tableau teases with a
hint of a narrative—the viewer
is left to ponder whether or not
the artist approaches his model
with hand extended in order to
ensure the correct proportions
for his painting or to engage in
activities of a different sort.

ATTRIBUTED TO HERBERT GLEASON
Boston, Massachusetts
Ship's Figurehead
c. 1865
wood, paint, and metal
76 × 20 × 26″
14 1/2″ lacing board
The Mariner's Museum,
Newport News, Virginia

(left) Representing the mythical
Galatea, who was sculpted from
stone into human flesh by her
beloved Pygmalion, this rare
figurehead embodied the identity of the ship it adorned.
Infused by neoclassical
grandeur, her strength is soft-
ened by the subtly sensuous
appearance of one bare breast.

ARTIST UNKNOWN
Lake Champlain, New York
Ice Fishing Rod
c. 1860
wood
22 1/4 × 2 1/4 × 2 3/4″
Private Collection

(below and opposite) The voluptuous curves that define the
shape of this carved ice fishing
rod, or "jiggle-stick," add both
visual and tactile pleasure to the
act of fishing. The artist has
transformed a mundane utilitarian object into an exquisite
sculpture that is meant to be
experienced from all angles.
The movement implied by this
nude's outstretched arms—she
appears to be diving—is made
even more dramatic when one
imagines the rod in use.

ARTIST UNKNOWN
● *Daguerreotype*
c. 1852
3 1/4 × 2 3/4″
Private Collection

(opposite) Known as "the mirror with the memory," the daguerreotype was the forerunner of modern photography. This medium allowed one-of-a-kind images to be produced on silver-coated copper plates through a process of exposure. While most daguerreotypes were portraits, **this** medium was also put to less predictable uses. This rare, up-close daguerreotype of a vagina is rather shocking, considering the time in which it was produced. But the artistry involved—implicit in the nature of the daguerreotype, and explicit when one considers the added process of hand tinting employed here—is not to be ignored. What might initially seem like a graphic or even pornographic spectacle is actually quite subjective and intimate.

ARTIST UNKNOWN
● *Woman with Pig*
19th century
bronze plaque
4 × 7 1/4″
The Kinsey Institute for
Research in Sex, Gender
and Reproduction,
Bloomington, Indiana

This bronze tableau provides a glimpse into a fantasy of bestiality. A reclining nude woman spreads her legs, thereby allowing access to an interested pig. This work is marked by eroticism and humor in equal measure.

ARTIST UNKNOWN
● *Couple*
19th century
iron bas-relief plaque
2 1/2 × 2 × 1/4″
The Kinsey Institute for
Research in Sex, Gender
and Reproduction,
Bloomington, Indiana

This relief tableau provides an unusual view of lovemaking. The horseshoe-shaped frame and the positioning of this couple seem calculated to charge our own viewing experience with a hint of voyeurism.

ARTIST UNKNOWN
● *Woman with an Ear of Corn*
19th century
cast-iron plaque
3 × 4 1/4 × 1/2″
The Kinsey Institute for
Research in Sex, Gender
and Reproduction,
Bloomington, Indiana

This cast-iron bas-relief plaque conjures up an example of creativity in the service of autoeroticism. A woman is depicted putting an ear of corn to a most unconventional use.

ARTIST UNKNOWN
Found in New England
Single-shot .22 Rim Fire Rifle
c. 1880
wood, steel, brass cutouts
28 1/4" long
Collection of Jonathan Holstein

(opposite) The art of rifle embellishment dates as far back as the introduction of the weapon itself. Indulging in a bit of Victorian erotica, this artist has capitalized on the sex appeal of the nineteenth century's favorite item of female anatomy—the well-shaped leg. This motif appears repeated in a sequence along the body of the rifle and again above the trigger, in each case presented to the viewer by a pointing hand. The result is racy but not bawdy, underscoring the gentlemanly sporting purpose of the weapon itself.

ARTIST UNKNOWN
Naughty Nellie, Bootjack
19th century
cast iron
9 1/2 × 4 1/2 × 2 1/2"
Private Collection

Once used as a bootjack, this utilitarian object, already erotic in nature, has been transformed into a delightful objet d'art. Designed to aid a gentleman with the act of removing his boots, this figurative tool has become an available, Rubenesque blonde, with the magic of paint. *(See page 24 for a detail.)*

ARTIST UNKNOWN
Indian Clubs
c. 1880–1890
polychromed wood
27″ high; 15 lbs.
Collection of Alice and
Ronald Hoffman

(below, with detail opposite) An exercising craze in the United States from 1862 through the 1930s, "Indian" club swinging was not, however, indigenous to this country. A popular form of recreation and strength building in nineteenth-century India, the practice of club swinging—which involved the rigorous, ordered, calisthenic manipulation of two clubs at once—was adapted by the British army as part of its own training regimen during this time. In 1861, the advocate of physical culture S. D. Kehoe witnessed a club-swinging exhibition in England and soon after introduced this practice to the American public, successfully manufacturing and marketing a refined version of the British model. These Victorian-era free weights were handmade as well as mass-produced, and were often embellished with a variety of images. Although the nude pictured in the detail opposite appears quite modern in hairstyle and demeanor, her proportions are timeless. The artist has cleverly matched the contours of the surface with those of her generous figure. This particular example suggests its gentleman user's purpose for exercising in the first place.

ARTIST(S) UNKNOWN
Mirrors and Advertising Pieces
c. 1890–1920
tin
circles: 1 3/4 × 2″
rectangles: 2 × 3″
Collection of Susan Parrett
and Rod Lich

The women that adorn these small "Thumb Girl" pieces and advertisements reflect the fashions and tenor of their time. Easily accessible and portable, such items mark the advent of pop-cultural erotica. Yet what look initially to be rather chaste images change radically when one covers each lady's head with a thumb and rotates each image 180 degrees.

54

From the Roaring Twenties to the free-love sixties, cultural revolutions expanded America's sexual awareness, inspiring generations of artists to explore erotica.

The first two decades of the twentieth century saw the full-blown emergence of sexual trends that had been put in motion—in theory and extremely limited practice—toward the end of the nineteenth century. Sexual theorists began to push the social envelope, **challenging the restrictive Victorian mores** that had come to define nineteenth-century life. As the seminal writings of Sigmund Freud became available in America, the notion of an all-important sexual drive began to gain currency among intellectuals. The progressive ideas of Havelock Ellis echoed those of Freud: Ellis held that sexual activity was the most important aspect of human life, and that it was to be pursued whenever possible for good health and well-being. The embrace of a freer sexuality by pro-sex radicals during the Gilded Age was to bloom, by the twenties, into reality on the level of mass culture.

The increasingly liberal approach toward sexuality that was to determine the nature of life in pre–War America was not only the result of ideas, but of massive economic and **social changes that were sweeping the nation.** The emergence of a consumer culture introduced into the public sphere that which had previously remained a matter of privacy. Social interactions between the sexes, which had earlier been carefully guarded by family and community, went largely unregulated, giving rise to **unprecedented potential for pre- and extramarital social and sexual intercourse between the sexes.** Commercially driven forums for social activities—dance halls, penny arcades, movie theaters, and the like—encouraged the pursuit of pleasure, and the burgeoning mass media drove this message home to the American people. Hollywood movies featuring both male and female heartthrobs, risqué dime-store novels, speakeasies, sweaty jazz halls, and, above all, advertising—these new, predominantly youth-oriented branches of popular culture confirmed and hastened the liberal direction that American sexuality would take in the twentieth century. And despite periodic setbacks, both economic (two world wars and a depression) and moral (the resurgence of conservative **"family values"** in the fifties, and not to mention more recently in the eighties and nineties), these new developments were here to stay.

This shift in the social climate was reflected in the work of academically trained and self-taught artists alike. During the first decades of the century, a raw and often graphic realism flourished in mainstream art, and this was echoed in its myriad margins. In self-taught painting, and sculpture, and in the ever-popular genre of sexual novelties, the influence of pop-cultural erotic imagery was all-pervasive.

Popular **erotic images from movies, magazines, and advertisements**—especially that of the alluring bathing beauty—were transformed into highly personal and increasingly frank sexual statements by wood-carvers, tinkerers, doodlers, Sunday painters, visionaries, and many other self-taught talents whose names are lost to us today. Comedic artworks and movable novelties spoofed popular comic-strip characters and pushed sexual humor to new extremes. The accessibility of electric tools enabled **tattoo artists** to indelibly etch graceful, and sometimes not so graceful, nudes onto the muscled arms of working-class men, and when the circus came to town, sexy billboard beauties announced the exotic and erotic pleasures on view under the big top. **Prison inmates fashioned lurid fantasies** out of readily available materials, and soldiers in both world wars incised visions of feminine beauty onto spent shell casings. World War II (and, later, Korean War) flying aces went into battle counting on the Vargas-inspired **pinup girls** painted on their planes to bring them courage and good luck.

In addition to these rich and varied traditions of erotica that come to us largely as anonymous contributions, the first half of the twentieth century saw the emergence of several recognized self-taught artists for whom the erotic was, to some degree, an important theme. Achilles G. Rizzoli rendered fantastically detailed and documented imaginary architectural edifices that symbolized personal sexual experiences. The prolific poet, painter, sculptor, and photographer Eugene Von Bruenchenhein produced thousands of black-and-white photographs of his **wife posed seminude** in lush, exotic settings. Once-institutionalized Justin McCarthy painted lush, expressive odes to the female figure, a topic that was also central to the retired New York City tailor Morris Hirshfield, whose uniquely flat, decorative style won him the admiration of mainstream modern artists and curators in the late thirties and early forties.

Reactions against what was perceived to be the **loosening of American morals** were widespread during the squeaky-clean post war baby-boom era of economic and reproductive prosperity, but this new wave of cultural restrictions was exploded by the social revolutions beginning in the late sixties. Civil rights movements for women and people of color were accompanied by what has become known as the **sexual revolution,** a movement in favor of freedom of sexual expression for heterosexuals and homosexuals alike. The youth culture that called for sexual freedom in the face of their parents' values was encouraged and confirmed by all aspects of popular culture, which by now included a **flourishing pornography industry.** What began as a relatively limited radical faction of free-love hippies eventually pervaded every level of American life. Although somewhat slowed by the onset of both **AIDS** and the renewed efforts of the **religious right,** the sexualizing of American culture has continued apace in the media-saturated, hyper-aware nineties.

These **newfound sexual freedoms** inspired expression in mainstream art, from the naked antics of performance artists in the late sixties and seven-

ties, to the more recent porn-appropriations of Jeff Koons, as well as in the politically oriented work of feminists, gays, and lesbians. But a freer sexuality has also been reflected on a grassroots level, in a variety of self-taught milieux. In rural America, the traditional, communal efforts of folk artists have gradually been replaced by untutored artists recognized for their individual artistic achievements, which often include erotica.

Self-taught artists who have become especially known for their erotic imagery include Steven Ashby, Henry and Georgia Speller, and Mose Tolliver. Other self-taught artists associated with the folk milieu who have addressed **sexual themes** include Sam Doyle, Miles Carpenter, James Harold Jennings, Edgar Tolson, and David Butler. All of these these artists have made vital contributions to the pluralistic history of erotic art.

In the work of untrained artists who have been, for better or worse, classified as "outsiders"—eccentrics, isolates, or the mentally ill—one can also find sexual themes expressed. This is true of the images and scribblings of the isolate Royal Robertson, and the figural drawings and writings of Dwight Mackintosh, who has been institutionalized for most of his life.

The diverse population of immigrants who have come to this country during the twentieth century has yielded many self-taught talents, in whose artwork one can find a variety of **erotic expressions.** Cuban-born Pucho Odio and the late German-born Gustave Klumpp both called New York City home; erotic themes may be found in both the lively wood carvings of the former and the naively painted figures of the latter.

Whether rural or urban, male or female, unknown or famous, all of these artists are linked by a common commitment to express their sexuality through a plurality of artistic modes that transcend reductive categories. More than simply exciting and entertaining, their achievements help to give us a better understanding of ourselves.

ARTIST UNKNOWN
• *Trench Art*
c. 1917
brass shell casing
13 ¾ × 3 ⅜″
Private Collection

This object represents a truly
unique genre in American popular art, aptly named trench
art — a kind of latter-day scrimshaw in which metal shell
casings have replaced a whale's
ivory. Born of the isolation and
stress of battle, this form of
expression was practiced by
American soldiers on the front
lines of both world wars. This
shell casing bears an incised
nude pictured mid-stride, naively rendered but graceful and
sensuous nonetheless.

60

ARTIST UNKNOWN
Ohio
• *Miss Moller*
c. 1910
polychromed pine
19 ¼ × 7 ½ × 3 ½″
Private Collection

(opposite) Frozen in the middle
of a graceful, yet decidedly
non-balletic, move, this
dancer's strength of both body
and gesture bespeaks a uniquely modern attitude. Likely
inspired by contemporary
developments in the field of
dance, the artist has explored
the appeal of the female body
in motion, infusing the dancer
with self-confidence, as well
as with what must have then
been an unprecedented sense
of sexual freedom.

NATIVE AMERICAN
(CHEROKEE)
• *Pipe Bowl*
1916
catlinite
6 × 2 ¼″
National Museum of the
American Indian, Smithsonian
Institution, New York

(left) One of the more explicit
examples of Native American
erotica, this carved pipe presents a threesome engaged in
various sexual activities. A
woman is shown performing
fellatio on a man in front of
her, while she is penetrated
from behind by a second man.
As these activities would no
doubt have been considered
scandalous by a white audience, they were a natural part
of the Plains Indian's sexual
repertoire, free as it was of the
stigma of imported prudishness.

ARTIST UNKNOWN
● *Silhouette Sticks*
1900
wood
6 3/4 × 1"
Collection of Instinctuals,
Alexandria, Virginia

The carver of this pair of silhouette shapes has exploited the
possibilities of both negative
and positive space to create an
optical illusion borne of neces-
sity. As in the case of most
erotic novelties, the need to
conceal gave rise to new explo-
rations of form. These two
wooden sticks *(left)* appear at
first to be beautiful, abstract
forms, but when held in front of
a direct light source, they cast
more anatomically specific
shadows *(opposite)*. The result
is an intimate scene between a
man and a woman, becoming
visible only to those who know
how to manipulate this effect.

63

ARTIST UNKNOWN
Minnesota
September Morn
early 20th century
paint and varnish on pine
9 1/4 × 3 × 2″
Collection of Louis and
Colleen Picek

This articulated novelty blends
humor with a frank sexuality.
Its development from "before"
to "after" is as much a spoof on
sexual modesty as it is a blatant
striptease. Surprisingly, the very
crude rendering of face, figure,
and movement add to this figure's raw sex appeal.

ARTIST UNKNOWN
Woodbridge, New Jersey
Woodbridge Figures
c. 1920
polychromed wood
tallest figure: 7 × 2 × 1 5/8″
Private Collection

(opposite) Not much is known
about these quirky, fecund figures, a limited number of which
were excavated from beneath a
gas station in Woodbridge, New
Jersey. It is believed that they
were produced and used in
rituals by a fertility cult; a
number of their attributes
support this thesis. The head
of each figure is hollow, and
the adult figures contain a
removable penis or vagina. This
group of two adults, one male
and one female, and two children, form a small family unit.
Their pinched faces, tall boots,
ample proportions, and lack of
arms all contribute to a singu-
larly uncanny sexuality.

W. YERRICK
Bathing Beauty
c. 1910
watercolor on paper
12 × 15 1/2″
Private Collection

(top left) Leaning forward to reveal
maximum cleavage, this naive take
on the popular genre of the bathing beauty exudes a clumsy eroticism. Sporadic attempts at perspective and anatomy only serve to
enhance the inviting nature of this
modern Rubenesque beauty.

ARTIST UNKNOWN
Bird Box
early 1900s
polychromed wood and wire
1 3/4 × 3 1/2 × 1 1/4″
The Kinsey Institute for Research
in Sex, Gender and Reproduction,
Bloomington, Indiana

(bottom left) Presenting an amusing
scenario involving an amorous pair
of birds, this object offers comic
insight into human sexual relations.
When the box is in a closed position, a single, female bird perches
on its lid, minding her own business. Yet when one slides the lid
forward, an eager mate pops out
and proceeds, rather unceremoni-
ously, to mount her.

ARTIST UNKNOWN
Buffalo, New York
Two Women
c. 1920
wood
15 × 26 × 17 1/2″
Collection of Lenny, Nancy,
and Jessie Kislin

(opposite) This sculptural group is
believed to have been carved by a
cult leader in Buffalo. The artist
has chosen to create a variation on
a classical sculptural theme—the
pietà. Charged with forbidden sexuality, this scene is set at the
water's edge; one woman swoons
under her lover's caress. Although
many such lesbian images are created for the entertainment of men,
this work, surprisingly sensitive to
the subject, is both erotically and
emotionally convincing.

ARTIST UNKNOWN
New England
Reclining Nude
c. 1920–1930
relief carving, wood with
varnish
12 1/2 × 24 × 3 1/2″
Ricco/Maresca Gallery,
New York

(opposite) This elegant tableau
is charged with erotic mystery.
Reclining on a sofa, a nude
woman appears to be lost in a
daydream, and judging by the
placement of her right hand, it
is likely that the dream is of a
sexual nature. Above the couch
appear portrait medallions of
two men—perhaps they are the
subjects of her erotic reverie.
The process of fantasizing that
this work gently represents
delivers a clever commentary
on the viewer's own implicit
voyeurism.

ARTIST UNKNOWN
Madam Queens Beauty Shoppe
1920
painted wood, cloth
4 1/2 × 6 1/2 × 4″
Collection of Richard Merkin

(right, top, and bottom) This
scene mixes a vaudevillian
sense of humor with bawdy
sexuality. Typical of the genre
of novelty toys, the setup
involves a hidden component,
which, when opened, delivers
the erotic punch line. When the
side of the Madam Queens [sic]
Beauty Shoppe is closed
(top), the scene is a tame one;
once opened *(bottom)*, the
viewer becomes privy to the
clandestine, backroom sexual
relations already underway.

ARTIST UNKNOWN
Bathing Beauty
c. 1930
pine
13 3/4 × 5 × 4"
Private Collection

(below) Evidence of a crude attempt to bring to life the classical bathing beauty, this carving nevertheless bears an erotic aura all its own. Despite—or perhaps because of—its very rough-hewn look, this figure effectively suggests, with perky modernity, the sensuality of the female figure.

HENRY FAJEN
Lake Huntington, New York
● *The Fox Chase/Whoopy*
c. 1930
sign, paint on wood
9 × 28 × ³/₄″
Private Collection

(left) Probably executed by a
sign painter on the back of an
old sign, these scenes address
the issue of communication
between the sexes. In "The Fox
Chase," the artist imagines an
unlikely encounter between a
bathing beauty and a gentleman
dressed for the hunt, a rather
clumsy pun that equates one
kind of hunting with another. In
"Whoopy," a man instructs his
son about the ways of the
world in the presence of three
frolicking beach nymphs. In
their primitivism, both quirky
narratives—replete with pop-
cultural imagery of the day—
provide a highly personal view
of sexuality.

"MH"
● *Three Women at the Beach*
1931
polychromed wood
21 ¹/₄ × 31 ³/₄ × 1 ⁷/₈″
Marvill Collection

(bottom left) From Botticelli's
Primavera, to Matisse's *The
Dance*, the image of dancing
women, hands linked, has
become etched into the collec-
tive art-historical unconscious.
This painted relief carving offers
up a decidedly modern version
of the theme of the three
Graces. Covered neither with
flowing gowns nor even with
contemporary bathing suits, the
stark, unidealized manner in
which these ladies have been
rendered might be described
not as nude, with the delicacy
that this term implies, but rather
as naked, connoting another,
more frank kind of eroticism.

72

ARTIST UNKNOWN
Hand Toy
c. 1920s–1930s
wood
4 × 6 ¼″
Forager House Collection

(top left) This small, handheld novelty is operated like a pistol. By pulling a trigger, the man springs into action, while the woman bends to receive him. There is more than a little humor to be found in the equation of this particular position, which suggests the same level of sexual aggression as that of firing a gun.

ARTIST UNKNOWN
Hand Toy
c. 1920s–1930s
plywood, pine, and paint
9 × 7 × 1 ¼″
Forager House Collection

(bottom left) In the case of this handheld toy, the equation between sex and shooting a gun is explicit. Two men are presented in an act of anal penetration, one dominant and the other submissive. The fact that the gun's trigger activates their relations augments the eroticism of this work with a lesson on the dynamics of sexual power.

ARTIST UNKNOWN
Ohio
Nude Couple
c. 1920
polychromed wood
8 ½ × 6 ¼ × 4 ½″
Private Collection

(opposite) Although they are not shown engaged in the act of intercourse, the relationship between this rough-hewn pair is nevertheless sexually charged. They stride in unison, and one wonders if the woman is leading the man (with erection in tow), or if he is indeed pursuing her. This ambiguity adds a depth of meaning that is surprising to find in so simple a work of art.

ARTIST UNKNOWN
Ohio
Jiggs
c. 1930
glazed ceramic sewer tile
7 1/2 × 2 3/4"
Collection of Susan Parrett
and Rod Lich

(left) Here, a popular comic-strip character has been caught with his pants down. The artist has fashioned an irreverent image of the henpecked Jiggs (of Jiggs and Maggie fame), which probably wouldn't have gained approval from newspaper censors of the 1930s.

ARTIST UNKNOWN
Man in a Barrel
c. 1920
4 × 2 × 2"
painted wood
Collection of Susan Parrett
and Rod Lich

(below) The man-in-the-barrel is a classic erotic novelty. Covered with the barrel, he is harmless enough; once the barrel is pulled off, he springs into action. Toys like this one poke fun at the high visibility of male desire.

ARTIST UNKNOWN
Indiana
Apron
1930s
cotton, and calico
15 3/4 × 18″
Collection of Susan Parrett
and Rod Lich

ARTIST UNKNOWN
Western Pennsylvania
His and Hers Pot Holders
1930s
gingham
8 1/4 × 7″
Collection of Susan Parrett
and Rod Lich

Very likely made and used by
women, these pieces add spice
to the domestic setting.
(top) Quite amusing are two gender specific pot holders—his and
hers. Although artworks in their
own right, these objects take on
new meaning when one imagines them put to use in the
kitchen. *(right)* Similarly unusual
is this "well-hung" apron—perhaps it provided the wearer with
a sense of comic relief as she
went about her tasks.

ARTIST UNKNOWN
Acquired in California
Barrel People
c. 1935
wood
3 1/2″
The Ames Gallery,
Berkeley, California

(right) These charmingly crude
novelties are truly like no
others. Although they follow the
familiar "before" and "after"
sequence of similar pop-up toys,
this pair packs a potent surprise.
When covered with their barrel-
like components, these male and
female companion figures seem
relatively tame, but when the
pieces are raised, each comes
alive with a prominent erection.
The humor, of course, lies in the
fact that the male, and not his
female partner, must confront a
considerable case of penis envy.

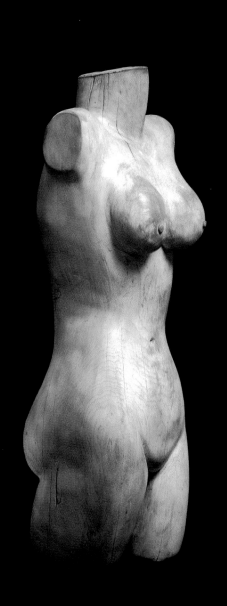

ARTIST UNKNOWN
(PROBABLY A LUMBERJACK)
Maine
Venus
c. 1930
wood (cedar?)
28 1/2 × 10 3/4 × 10″
Collection of Steve Miller

(opposite) Carved to provide voluptuous companionship during lonely times, this rural American *Venus de Milo* consists of just the bare essentials. Providing more than simply a visual comfort, noticeable wear and tear on this figure's breasts attests to an intimate relationship between the unknown lumberjack Pygmalion and his wooden Galatea. The artist's emphasis on the breasts, torso, and lower part of the female body, to the exclusion of all else, gives this sculpture a certain erotic intensity.

ACHILLES G. RIZZOLI
(1896 –1981)
San Francisco
Primal Glimse
April 12, 1936
ink on paper
54 × 26″
The Ames Gallery,
Berkeley, California

The Swiss-Italian artist Achilles G. Rizzoli was inspired by otherworldly visions to render fantastical architectural plans, complete with written commentary, that were often personifications of specific people or symbolic of different experiences. It is no mistake that this exquisitely detailed drawing of a tower is phallic shaped, a tribute to, or, in the artist's words, a "primal glimse" into, his own experience of orgasm. For Rizzoli, the successive elevations of this edifice, meticulously annotated with sexually suggestive language at the top left, serve the purpose of "interpreting the reactions experienced during that incomparable moment," which apparently transpired between two and four P.M. on April 12, 1936.

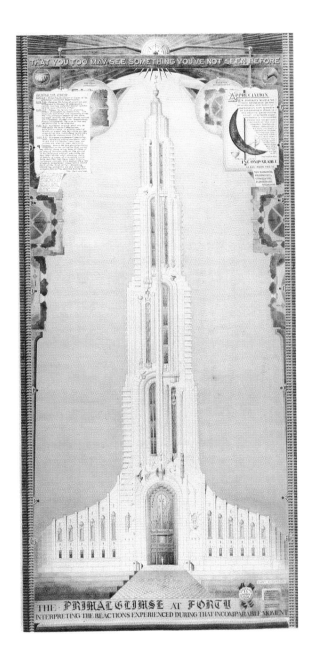

ARTIST UNKNOWN
Reclining Lady
c. 1920
polychromed pine
13 × 25 × 17″
The Marvill Collection

Here, the classic pinup girl has been transformed from a pop-cultural icon into a more personal statement. Inclined toward the viewer, elbow on knee, her pose has precedents in popular imagery, especially advertising. Yet this hand-carved work has rendered a modern, mass-media archetype into an intimate artwork.

ARTIST UNKNOWN
Cigar Box
c. 1930–1940
6 × 8 1/2 × 2 1/4″
Collection of Charles G. Haak

(opposite) This rare piece of automated erotica was discovered hidden inside a secret hole in an elderly man's mattress after he'd passed away. Jury-rigged from simple materials including a cigar box—a phallic entendre in itself—its humor hinges on the artist's clever recycling of pop-cultural detritus. To the right, a nude figure lies on a bed; by inserting a coin in a slot beneath her, a mechanism causes a mechanical penis to engage her in frantic, albeit robotic, intercourse. Appropriated text appearing throughout this tableau attests to its erotic nature.

 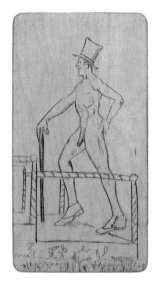

"MARTY"
Ye Olde Maide
1937
incised plywood
7 1/4 × 4 × 1/4″
Collection of Richard Merkin

The artist has incised this image onto the surface of two ply-wood panels by means of a precise burning tool. Together, the two parts to this enjoyable diptych form a simple but witti-ly rendered narrative. A sartori-ally sparse gentleman is shown approaching a brothel, where he receives a warm welcome at the door. This is a quaint, nos-talgic fantasy about sexual rela-tions in an earlier and—so it seems to the mind of the artist—less complicated time.

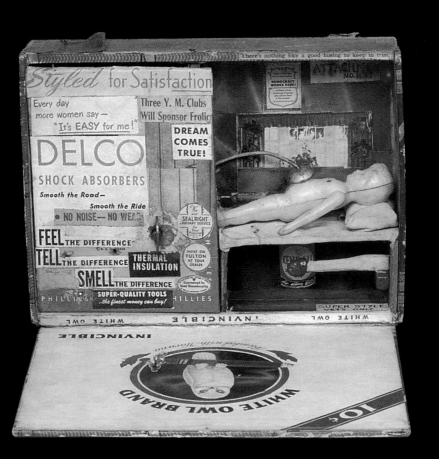

ARTIST UNKNOWN
WWII Airplane Nose Art:
Miss Behavin'
c. 1940
paint on metal

ARTIST UNKNOWN
WWII Airplane Nose Art:
Double Trouble
c. 1940
paint on metal

ARTIST UNKNOWN
WWII Airplane Nose Art:
Our Gal
c. 1940
paint on metal
U.S. Air Force Museum,
Dayton, Ohio

(left, top to bottom) Painted onto
the nose and fuselage of combat
aircraft of both World War II
and the Korean War, sexy
images of women, accompanied
by nicknames emblazoned in
dramatic lettering, served a variety of functions. Like the bare-
breasted ladies of the previous
century's sailing ships, each one
of these modern pin-ups—
inspired by Vargas, the latest
Hollywood starlet, or the girl
next door—was not only a per-
sonification of the aircraft's
identity, but also its symbolic
protection, as well as a morale
booster and fantasy fuel for the
pilot and his crew. Together, the
combination of text and image
that exemplifies this genre
communicates a double
message of sex and war, eroticism and courage, and pleasure
and human destruction.
(top) Posing in classic pinup
fashion, this woman's name is a
pun that warns of the daring of
the plane and her crew.
(center) This dialectic is evident
in an image of a bare-breasted
woman in midflight, driven forward by propellers attached to
her breasts. Here, the artist has
wittily equated destructive
attributes with erotic ones.
(bottom) Finally, a term of
endearment identifying a crew's
symbolic protectress also loving-
ly names their craft.

ARTIST(S) UNKNOWN
WWII Airplane Nose Art : (clock-
wise) Slightly Dangerous; Buzz
Job; Miss Laid; Sack Time Sal II;
Fast Company; Near Miss
c. 1940
paint on metal
(clockwise): National Air and
Space Museum, Washington,
D.C.; U.S. Air Force Museum,
Dayton, Ohio; U.S. Air Force
Museum, Dayton, Ohio;
National Air and Space
Museum, Washington, D.C.;
National Air and Space
Museum, Washington, D.C.;
National Air and Space
Museum, Washington, D.C.

(opposite) Examples of airplane
nose art are as artistically
diverse as were the artists
who painted them. These six
works illustrate the range of
sensibilities that come together
in this genre to create images
both sexy and sweet. At top
left, a bare-breasted starlet
cheerfully embodies her plane's
raison d'être. The tableau featured to the right, in which a
bee's sexual intentions imitate
an airplane's attack dive, is as
humorous as it is deadly serious. At center left, a bathing
beauty attests to a close call,
while to the right, a country
girl in cutoffs appears to invite
more than wartime activity.
More dramatic is the athletic
figure at bottom left, which
boldly equates airspeed with
sexual appetite, and to the right
stands a seductive siren whose
bedroom eyes spell disaster to
lovers and enemies alike.

EUGENE VON BRUENCHENHEIN
(1910–1983)
Milwaukee, Wisconsin
Photographs of Marie
c. 1940–1950
black-and-white photographs
8 × 10″
Carl Hammer Gallery,
Chicago, Illinois

The artist Eugene Von
Bruenchenhein worked in a
variety of media, but the
thousands of black-and-white
photographs he took and devel-
oped of his wife, Eveline, (who
eventually came to use the
name Marie) stand as a testimony to his fascination with the
female body. The manner in
which he posed Marie often
downplays her individuality in
order to draw out a more universal sexuality. *(top)* Set
against a plain background, and
with minimal decorative detail
to distract the viewer, a certain
openness in Marie emerges in
this picture, adding a sense of
immediacy to its romantic, erotic allure. In another photograph
(bottom right), Marie is displayed, arms behind her head,
against a rich, patterned back-
drop. The play of light and several pearl necklaces divide her
body into abstracted areas, visually linking its sensuous curves
to the floral motifs behind. The
same decorative impulse is at
work in a third picture
(bottom left). With her head cast
down and body in full view,
Marie becomes an anonymous
Odalisque, frozen in a moment
of timeless languor.

82

MINNIE EVANS
(1892–1987)
Wilmington, North Carolina
• *Woman*
c. 1943
graphite and crayon on paper
7 1/4 × 5″
Luise Ross Gallery, New York

Born and raised in North
Carolina, Minnie Evans worked
as a "sounder" hawking
seafood, and later as gatekeep-
er to the gardens of a sumptu-
ous estate. Experiencing visions
from an early age, Evans was
called to make art in 1935; the
only teacher she credits is God.
Her oeuvre, which consists of
exquisitely rendered abstractive
interpretations of Revelation
and other religious subjects,
dates from the 1940s to the
1970s. This early work offers a
look at Evans's favored facial
type, as well as her penchant
for graceful floral abstraction.
Yet in this image, the swirling
lines that elsewhere bear no
more than an implicit fecundity
explicitly outline the anatomical
features of this otherworldly
goddess. The artist has, without
pretension, equated sexuality
with the divine.

84

ARTIST UNKNOWN
Frenchtown, New Jersey
Spoon Figures
Late 1940s
aluminum with copper rivets
4″ high
Kelter-Malce, New York

Inspired by the isolated nature
of prison life and the limited
materials available there, this
novelty is a testimony to artistic
ingenuity. The artist has
fashioned the figures of two
lovers out of simple cafeteria
spoons; held together by several well-placed rivets, they may
be manipulated (as is demon-
strated by the left-to-right
sequence above) into an acro-
batic act of coitus.

ARTIST UNKNOWN
● *Book*
c. 1920
5 1/4 × 3 5/8″ (closed)
5 1/4 × 7 1/2″ (open)
Collection of Richard Merkin

Constructed out of hinged
paper cutouts, this novelty is
deceptively simple. By opening
the book's cover, an intimate
scene is revealed. A simple
back-and-forth manipulation
of a small tab sets the man's
figure into motion, while the
woman, wearing only a hat and
a smile, stands gazing into the
distance. A schematic rendering
of hairstyle and facial type
nevertheless conveys the fashion of the day.

ARTIST UNKNOWN
Flash
c. 1930
ink and watercolor on paper
48 × 10″
(each section 8 × 10″)
Collection of
Herbert Waide Hemphill, Jr.

(opposite, left) The hallowed art of tattooing has traditionally been enriched by erotica. This is an example of the way that a tattooer's "flash," or the sheets of illustration board or paper on which tattoo artists demonstrate their repertoire of images, might be displayed on the shop wall. Each of the six sections, or sheets, contains a lively composition in which dominant images are complemented by smaller ones, creating quite an eyeful. *(opposite, right)* One section from this sequence has been enlarged to reveal the wealth of erotica included in this artist's repertoire. At the center of the composition is an all-American Venus riding a butterfly. To the left at the top, a death's head is revealed to be a rather acrobatically displayed nude, a masterful example of visual trickery in the service of titillation.

LEONARD ("STONEY") L. ST. CLAIR
(1912–1980)
West Virginia
Flash
c. 1940
ink and watercolor on paper
9 3/4 × 11 3/4″
Collection of
Herbert Waide Hemphill, Jr.

This example of flash combines tamer images, such as a diapered tot and a dove, with two racier ones, camouflaged by means of trick imagery. On the upper left, an Indian brave's face becomes a seductive nude; on the upper right, Sigmund Freud appears to be contemplating the same thing. Such images remind one that tattooing has traditionally been favored by men.

JUSTIN McCARTHY
(1892–1977)
Pennsylvania
Female Nude
c. 1940
watercolor on paper
10 × 8″
Epstein/Powell Gallery,
New York

Green Stockings
c. 1940
watercolor on paper
9 × 11″
Epstein/Powell Gallery,
New York

Justin McCarthy, a recluse and an extraordinary painter, wasn't "discovered" until 1960. This would-be law student suffered a nervous breakdown and was institutionalized from 1915 to 1920. Upon his release, McCarthy lived in his family's Pennsylvania mansion and quickly became a prolific draftsman, but it wasn't until the forties that he began to paint. His themes were quintessentially American—sports, history, and Hollywood stars, among others. To be sure, women feature prominently in his oeuvre.
(top) In this painting, McCarthy explores the erotic possibilities of the nude in an explicit manner. A woman reclines, with legs spread, fully exposed to the viewer. The artist has skillfully used color to enhance her appeal—red defines her lips and cheeks, as well as her vagina. McCarthy's subtle artistry has transformed an otherwise candid image into a celebration of the female body.
(bottom) This watercolor displays McCarthy's talent for capturing a more subtle eroticism. A provocatively dressed woman bends down to pet a goose, a perfectly innocent gesture, that has, in McCarthy's hands, become unmistakably seductive.

ARTIST UNKNOWN
New York
Nude Carving
c. 1940
polychromed pine
10 1/2 × 5 1/4″ × 13 3/4″
Collection of Steve Miller

(opposite) This remarkably animated sculpture is both charming and intensely sexual. Taking his cue from the commercial pinup genre, the artist has forged in this figure a mixture of modesty and seductiveness. Although she sits with her legs crossed, she wears nothing but a pair of pumps and fondles one of her own breasts. In hairstyle, facial type, and the style of her shoes, she is a stereotype of her time period, but, at the same time, the artist has drawn out a universal and timeless appeal.

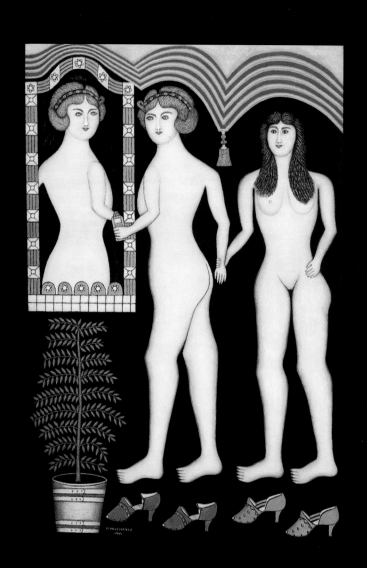

MORRIS HIRSHFIELD
(1872–1946)
New York
Inseparable Friends
1941
oil on canvas
60 ¹/₈ × 40 ¹/₈″
The Museum of Modern Art,
New York, The Sidney and
Harriet Janis Collection

Nude at the Window
1941
oil on canvas
54 × 30″
Private Collection

One of this country's most cele-
brated self-taught painters, Morris
Hirshfield has become known for
his fantastical compositions often
populated with beautiful ladies. A
Polish-Jewish émigré, Hirshfield
worked most of his life as a tailor
in New York City and began to
paint upon retiring in 1937. His
paintings, characterized by stylized
figuration and mesmerizing
abstract decoration, appealed to
aficionados of modern art—
Hirshfield was discovered by the
art dealer Sidney Janis, who included him in a group exhibition at the
Museum of Modern Art in 1939,
and arranged a solo show for the
artist there in 1943. *(right)* Here, a
simply rendered but nevertheless
voluptuous nude, who has just
removed her shoes, peers out from
behind rich drapery, providing the
viewer with a seemingly clandestine peek. This work derives its
charm from its playful sense of
harmless voyeurism, a theme that
was one of Hirshfield's favorites.
(opposite) In another painting,
Hirshfield explores an intimate liai-
son between two women. A nude
at the center is the object of several gazes—her own, her lover's, and
ours. Here, the artist gently provides insight into the erotic appeal
that lesbian encounters hold for
many men. Refraining from explicit
detail, Hirshfield has successfully
created a visually exciting tableau
charged with sexual expectation.

ARTIST UNKNOWN
Articulated Figure
c. 1950
painted wood
8 3/4 × 3 × 1 1/4″
Private Collection

(left) Crudely fashioned, this figure, with its jangling arms and legs, exudes a raw sexuality. Known as a limberjack, this toy was built to execute a jerky dance. By holding it from a stick attached behind and placing its feet upon a board that rests under one's thigh, the figure may be set to dancing simply by tapping the board. Painted almost entirely black, this work is likely the artist's awkward attempt to depict a black woman, and evokes an uncannily vaudevillian brand of humor. The breasts, painted a gaudy orange bordered by yellow, are both the visual and erotic focus of this piece, notwithstanding the ubiquitous red highlights announcing the presence of lips and shoes. Although ugly, this figure is a fascinating testimony to a rather eccentric notion of sexual entertainment.

ARTIST UNKNOWN
Kansas City, Missouri
Circus Banner: Snakes, Snakes
c. 1940
paint on canvas
92 × 116″
My Country's Folk Art,
Ridgewood, New Jersey

(opposite) Inviting potential circusgoers to embark on an exciting adventure, this banner mixes sexuality with pure exoticism. The result is an overdetermined fantasy. Two seminude women suggestively drape a giant snake around their bodies, its phallic nature underscored by its lurid, appropriately aimed hissing gesture. Here, a brazen kind of sexuality has been made acceptable under the guise of gypsylike exoticism—these ladies, like the highly physical circus itself, offer a safe, vicarious sexual encounter, if only of a visual nature.

BILL TRAYLOR
(1854–1949)
Montgomery, Alabama
• *Man*
1939–1942
paint on cardboard
10 × 8″
Private Collection

(top) Born into slavery in rural Alabama, Bill Traylor lived most of his life as a farmhand on the Traylor plantation. After his (approximately) twenty children were grown, Traylor moved to Montgomery in 1938, where he worked for a short time, eventually retiring due to bad health. Sleeping in the back of a funeral home, and spending his days sitting on the sidewalk, drawing, Traylor's presence came to the attention of a young white artist named Charles Shannon, who brought him art supplies and nurtured his talent. Traylor drew and later painted lively scenes on discarded cardboard, which recounted his memories of rural life or vividly related the activities of denizens of the black section of Montgomery. Marked by a careful observation of human nature, these works occasionally turned to sexually oriented subjects, often with a keen observational wit. This image, all the funnier for Traylor's trademark penchant for silhouetted figures, pictures a man in a compromising position. Whether he is masturbating or just relieving himself was only for Traylor to know for sure.

94

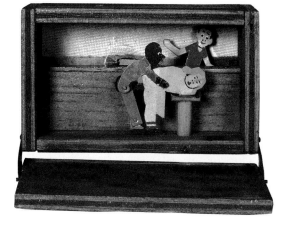

ARTIST UNKNOWN
• *Archie's Tavern*
c. 1940
wood and metal
2 1/2 × 4 × 2 1/2″
Collection of Richard Merkin

(bottom) This movable novelty is a pure delight. The lid of this box opens to reveal a quaint but erotic scene. A woman bends over a bar stool, while a man penetrates her from behind, to the amusement of the bartender. A hidden lever sets both male figures in motion; the bartender gestures happily, while the other man is set into frenetic copulation. This tableau's humor has a twist—the central pun is a confirmation of the legendary sexual prowess of the African American man.

ARTIST UNKNOWN (TINSMITH)
• *Stencils*
c. 1940
tin and copper
From 2 1/2″ to 4 1/2″ high
Collection of Susan Parrett and Rod Lich

(opposite) This set of stencils is decidedly unconventional. Used as templates for drawings, the number of sexual combinations that one might decide to create by translating these shapes onto paper is endless. Yet aside from their intended use, these objects are interesting and enigmatic in their own right. Seen alone, the exaggerated postures of the individual figures appears contorted, even painful—they might almost be parodies of the rigors of sexual intercourse. Nevertheless, it is difficult to deny their erotic dynamism.

NATIVE AMERICAN (HOPI)
Southwest
Kachina Doll
c. 1950–1960
polychromed cottonwood root
6 × 2³/₄ × 2¹/₂″
Collection of Charles G. Haak

Representations of spirits venerated by the Hopi people, kachina dolls have long helped to humanize and facilitate a better understanding of these otherworldly beings upon whose graces, it was (and is) believed, depend the lives of the community. Personifications of natural forces, kachina spirits are ritually venerated to ensure fertility of both the land and the people. This kachina doll represents one such spirit, Kokopelli, whose significance is easily identified—to believers and nonbelievers alike—by his primary attribute.

EDDIE OWENS MARTIN (SAINT EOM)
(1908–1986)
Three Details from Pasaquan
late 1950–1970
painted cement
dimensions variable
Pasaquan Society of the Marion
County Historical Society,
Buena Vista, Georgia

(right) The life of Eddie Martin was as colorful as the brightly painted visionary environment he built in Buena Vista, Georgia, during the second half of his life. Born in nearby Glen Alta, Martin struck out for New York City at the tender age of fourteen, where he led the life of a gay street hustler and a drug dealer, among other things. In 1935, during a bout of ill health, Martin had a vision that inspired him to investigate his spirituality, and soon after, he heard a voice declare: "You're gonna be the start of somethin' new, and you'll call yourself Saint EOM, and you'll be a *Pasaquoyan*— the first one in the world." The rich, culturally eclectic nature of Saint EOM's philosophy of "the hair and the beard"—unquestionably influenced by the vibrant cultural milieu in which he moved in New York—was echoed in the artwork he began to produce after his spiritual awakening. Yet although he exhibited his paintings at galleries, it was the grand, breathtaking compound he began building in 1957 that earned him recognition as an artist.

(above) Constructed on a four-acre plot of land he inherited after his mother's death, this environment, not surprisingly named *Pasaquan* by Saint EOM, is a virtual smorgasbord of decorative motifs and religious iconography, subsumed and reinvented by his own unifying vision. Consisting of various structures, wildly embellished walls, and freestanding, totemic figures, Pasaquan is subtly punctuated with erotica, as is evidenced in these male and female nudes.

98

SATURNINO PORTUONDO "PUCHO" ODIO
(1928–)
New York
● *Man and Guitar*
c. 1965
polychromed wood, wire
34 ½ × 15 x 4″
Private Collection

(far left) Pucho Odio was born in Cuba in 1928, and emigrated first to Canada and then to the United States in 1963. Experience as a laborer—especially as a carpenter—eventually provided him with valuable skills that he would later put to use as a wood-carver. This carved figure is but one of many works made by Odio to immortalize different members of his Cuban American community in New York. Like most of his figural works, this piece is simple yet witty. A man plays the guitar with his penis in full view, a wonderful equation of the musical instrument and the sexual organ, which speaks volumes about the notorious libido of musical performers.

ARTIST UNKNOWN
● *Hermaphrodite*
1960
wood
7 × 1″
The Kinsey Institute for Research in Sex, Gender and Reproduction, Bloomington, Indiana

(near left) Carved by a prison inmate, this work attests to the artist's lively and unusual sexual imagination. Assuming the sensuous curves of a woman's body, the figure nevertheless sports male genitalia. While the curious appeal of the hermaphrodite is ancient, this work is especially pertinent in today's context of gender bending and transsexualism. Another unsettling feature is this creature's lack of arms, making it appear relatively passive, a startling visual contrast to its prominent erection.

VICTOR JOSEPH GATTO
(1893–1965)
Hoboken, New Jersey
Burlesque Show
c. 1960
oil on canvas
14 × 18″
Epstein/Powell Gallery,
New York

(top right) Born and raised in New York's Little Italy, Victor Joseph Gatto always loved to draw, but it wasn't until 1938, after he had tried his hand at a number of professions, that he decided to become an artist. Gatto's paintings, whether portraits or lively scenes of horse and dog racing, are always marked by self-taught inventiveness. In this painting, the artist has cleverly created a scene that is equal parts narrative and witty metaphor. Stepping out from behind what appear to be curtains, an array of nude women venture onstage, each one engaged in her own seductive dance. Their audience consists of men's heads, each one perched atop a phallic protrusion. These penis-men look eagerly on, dwarfed by the women who perform for them. In this rather bizarre scenario, Gatto has provided a very telling take on relations between the sexes.

GEORGE MESISCO
Scarsdale, New York
Cradle of Love
c. 1950
embroidery on cardboard
5 × 6″
Epstein/Powell Gallery,
New York

(bottom right) This is a surprisingly erotic image to find in the medium of embroidery, normally a venue for lighter fare. A couple is depicted in the throes of passionate lovemaking, and it is difficult to determine where one figure ends and another begins. Yet as intense as this image is, it seems gentler than might be the case if rendered in another medium.

DANIEL PRESSLEY
(1918–1971)
New York
● *A Summer Day Chore*
c. 1965
polychromed wood
40 × 20″
Collection of Marcia Wilson

(opposite) A native of South Carolina, Daniel Pressley moved to New York City in the early forties. Although he recalled being interested in art as a child, it wasn't until 1962, when a serious illness curtailed his work as a plumber, that he turned to art-making as a full-time profession. Although an accomplished draftsman and painter, Pressley's forte was woodcarving, and he is best known for his relief carvings that depict scenes inspired by his often painful memories of the South, as well as by daily life in his African American community in New York City. This particular relief relates a casual eroticism. An amply endowed woman sits on a windowsill, while a man below busies himself with yardwork. With keen observation and a skillful hand, Pressley has added both humor and spice to the otherwise mundane.

JACK SAVITSKY
(1910–)
Pennsylvania
● *Nude*
c. 1960
oil on masonite
7 3/4 × 3 3/4″
Collection of Instinctuals,
Alexandria, Virginia

John "Jack" Savitsky spent most of his life working in the Pennsylvania coal mines. By the time his place of employment shut down in 1959, Savitsky had already contracted the deadly disease known as black lung, and chose to retire. At the suggestion of his son, Savitsky began to paint and soon became well known for his singular style and compelling scenes that brought to life both the beauty of his Pennsylvania environs as well as the hardships of mining life there. But Savitsky's repertoire is not limited to mining narratives—this voluptuous nude attests to the artist's versatility. Rendered at almost full length, this figure is painted in rich, warm tones, her seductiveness due as much to a precocious use of paint as to well-placed, evocative curves. This painting adds depth to the more popularly known masculine narratives that have characterized Savitsky's oeuvre.

A SUMMER DAY CHORE

THORNTON DIAL, SR.
(1928–)
Bessemer, Alabama
Lady with Fish
1991
graphite & watercolor on paper
22 × 30″
Collection of William Arnett

Two Women with Tiger
c. 1970
watercolor on paper
23 × 30″
Collection of Instinctuals,
Alexandria, Virginia

A native of Alabama, Thornton
"Buck" Dial, Sr., remembers
making "things," or mixed-
media assemblages, all his life.
Inspired by the skills and materials acquired while working a
variety of jobs, these objects
were dense fables through
which Dial, an African
American, expressed the vicissitudes of black history and black
life. Since 1987, the artist has
channeled these rich narratives
onto large-scale canvases, a
mode that he consistently
complements with fluid,
expressive works on paper that
are often tableaux of women
and animals. Sometimes these
images are wildly erotic.
(opposite) In this work, an
attenuated nude returns the
viewer's gaze, while at the bottom, a subtly phallic fish sets
the composition in balance.
With legs spread wide, her sensuality has been augmented by
the artist's knowing placement
of pink highlights. Even wilder
is another composition *(right)*,
in which a tiger appears to
be caught in an orgiastic
vortex with two nude women.
In Dial's allegorical lexicon,
the tiger often represents the
black man.

ARTIST UNKNOWN

ARTIST UNKNOWN
● *Prison Art*
1960
pencil and crayon on paper
8 1/2 × 5 1/2"
The Kinsey Institute for
Research in Sex, Gender
and Reproduction,
Bloomington, Indiana

(left) Prison art—art made by
prison inmates—has become a
popular genre within the field
of nonmainstream art, attracting
increasing attention from art
critics and collectors alike. With
plenty of time on their hands,
prisoners have, over the years,
produced significant works of
art; pen-and-ink drawing, for
the obvious reason that the
implements are easily acquired,
has been a popular medium.
One source of inspiration has
been the so-called genre of
"eight pagers," or sequential
comiclike drawings in sequence
that spoof popular comic
strips. This work is a witty
send-up of sexual inter-
course.

RICHARD TAYLOR
● *Soul Drane*
watercolor on cardboard
23 × 18 1/4"
The Tartt Gallery,
Washington, D.C.

(left) An unnerving mixture of
eroticism and violence, this
painting by death-row inmate
Richard Taylor proposes a
shower room showdown
between two supersexed
humans. In a clever composi-
tional strategy that involves an
imagined reflection and results
in near-abstract vertigo, the
artist provides different angles
from which to ogle the subjects'
oversize bodies. A man and a
woman face off—he wields a
shank-knife, and she, a
revolver—but despite the
impending mayhem that this
scene suggests, it is eerily shot
through with sexual possibility.

ARTIST UNKNOWN
● *Prison Art*
early 1960s
colored pencils on paper
individual images range from
between 8 1/2 × 7" to 9 1/4 × 7 1/2"
The Kinsey Institute for
Research in Sex, Gender
and Reproduction,
Bloomington, Indiana

(opposite) The isolation and
same-sex segregation that
define the prison experience
provide a limited outlet for sexual expression. Drawings such
as these have been a way for
inmates to express sexual fantasies. The sequence format
provides the viewer with a
vivid, vicarious experience that
is not unlike the effect of a
pornographic movie. In this
work, the artist has imagined a
scenario set in the infirmary.
The typically buxom nurse suc-
cumbs to the seduction of her
charge, and their impassioned
dialogue leads to various other
pulse-raising activities.

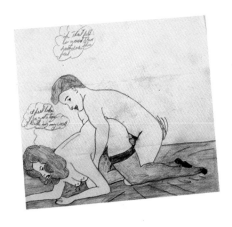

MICHAEL RINALDI
(1954–)
• *Incubus (Demon of Lust)*
colored pencil, ink, matt board
12 × 19 1/4″
Phyllis Kind Gallery, New York

• *Ice Cream on a Blue Monday*
1990
felt marker on board
11 1/2 × 14 1/2″
Phyllis Kind Gallery, New York

(top left) One prison artist who
has established a reputation for
himself outside of the standard
genre of comic-strip erotica is
Michael Rinaldi. His knack for
exploring the darker side of
human sexuality results in
uniquely disturbing imagery.
That his drawings are also visually rich adds to their power to
consistently hit a note of dis-
cord. In this work, the artist
updates a theme made popular
by the Romantic British painter
Henri Fusili—the incubus, or
demon, who sexually invades
women while they sleep.
Rinaldi's demon has sprouted
many hideously long penises,
which snake out and penetrate
women who appear to be
trapped helplessly in a swirling,
claustrophobic atmosphere. Yet
these women seem cooperative,
eager participants in this exces-
sive fantasy. *(bottom left)* In
another work, Rinaldi conflates
different kinds of greed. The
grotesque female figure depicted here slurps an unnaturally
colored ice-cream cone, while
fluid of the same color spouts
out of her breasts. With nothing
but felt marker, the artist has
transported erotic experience
into the realm of the uncanny.

MOSE TOLLIVER
(1919–)
Montgomery, Alabama
Sexual Fantasy
(Lady on a Scooter)
c. 1970s
house paint on plywood
24 7/8 × 18 3/4″
Collection of
Herbert Waide Hemphill, Jr.

Richard, Anton, and MoseT
1985
paint on latex rubber
42 × 71″
Gasperi Gallery, New Orleans

Few self-taught artists are as famous for the erotic component of their work as is Mose Tolliver. Born near Montgomery, Alabama, Tolliver, an African American, worked as a laborer most of his life until a fateful event changed his life forever—in the late sixties, while unloading furniture from a delivery truck, a load of marble crushed his legs, leaving him crippled for life. At the encouragement of his former employer, Tolliver began to paint in the early seventies, embarking on what has become an illustrious career as an artist. While he is known for paintings inspired by everyday life as well as by his imagination, he is a prolific painter of erotica.
(top) This work is a classic example of Tolliver's "Ladies on Scooters" theme. The smile on this lady's face is echoed by the upward curve of her splayed legs, while she rides upon what looks like a penis on wheels. Tolliver's penchant for the bawdy is played out in an orgy scene painted on the back of a rug *(bottom)*, in which the primary participants are well-known figures in the folk art world. Here, Tolliver has included himself as an observer, crutches and all, while caricatures of two friends are depicted living it up.

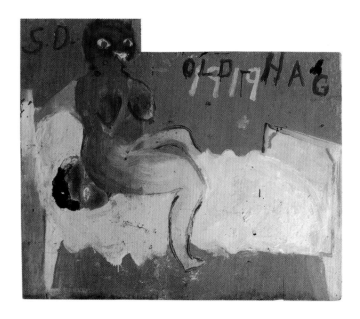

SAM DOYLE
(1906–1985)
St. Helena Island,
South Carolina
• *He/She*
1944–1980
enamel on tin
42 × 27″
Collection of
Louanne C. La Roche

• *Old Hag*
c. 1977
enamel on tin
48 × 36/41″
Collection of Robert A. Roth

The self-taught, African American painter Sam "Uncle Sam" Doyle was born and lived most of his life on St. Helena Island, off the coast of South Carolina. The island's isolation nurtured the rich African American traditions that have thrived there since the time of slavery, and the African-derived dialect of Gullah may still be heard there. Doyle's paintings—rough and vibrant compositions painted in enamel or latex on discarded corrugated roofing tin or wooden board—record and interpret this lively culture, as well as African American history in general. Among the denizens of his island were many eccentric figures whom Doyle loved to capture for posterity. *(top)* This work captures one such individual. The artist has cleverly expressed the dual nature of a person who was likely gay, bisexual, or a transvestite by literally representing both "sides" of his/her gender identity in a double caricature. *(bottom)* A second work depicts yet another citizen of St. Helena, who appears to have been a prostitute rather worse for the wear.

MILES B. CARPENTER
(1889–1985)
Waverly, Virginia
Devil
1972
paint on wood
17 1/2 × 7 1/2 × 11″
Collection of Martin and
Enid Packard

A native of Pennsylvania, Miles
Burkholder Carpenter lived
most of his life in Waverly,
Virginia. Carpenter's facility for
wood carving is no mystery—a
lifetime of experience working
at a sawmill provided him with
valuable skills with which to
actualize his innate artistic talent. His painted carvings are
often humorous indictments of
people in his community, but
religion has been an important
source of inspiration as well. In
this carving, Carpenter has set
his sights on the devil himself,
poking fun at the evil one's
virility, or lack thereof. Painted
bright red, and accompanied by
his dog, this devil may be fitted
with alternate sets of genitals,
enabling one to transform him
from an erect to a flaccid state,
and back again.

STEVEN ASHBY
(1904–1980)
Delaplane, Virginia
Woman and Centaur
c. 1960s–1970s
mixed media
7 1/2 × 9 × 2 1/8"
Collection of
Herbert Waide Hemphill, Jr.

Woman
1975
mixed media
6 1/4 × 10 3/4 × 6"
Collection of
Herbert Waide Hemphill, Jr.

Whirligig
1960s
mixed media
15 1/4 × 12 × 3 5/8"
Collection of
Herbert Waide Hemphill, Jr.

Steve Ashby was a self-taught master of three-dimensional erotica. Ashby did not begin making what he called his "fixing-ups" until his wife died in 1960 (he made less than two hundred in all). Each of these brilliantly jury-rigged mixed media figures has a personality all its own. Many fixing-ups bear witness to Ashby's lively sexual imagination. *(top left)* This work features a couple engaged in coitus, and a lever helps to set them in motion, making this activity more vivid.
(bottom left) Another work involves a nude with goggles for eyes, who displays herself for the viewer. She comes complete with a container that may be filled with water, which, when placed behind her genital area and poured through her "vagina" to the front, provides the viewer with the entertaining illusion that she is wetting herself.
(opposite) This is a raucous whirligig that best illustrates Ashby's keen sense of humor. When activated by the wind, the propeller's rotations cause the man to simultaneously fondle his female companion and himself. This is slapstick sexual humor at its best.

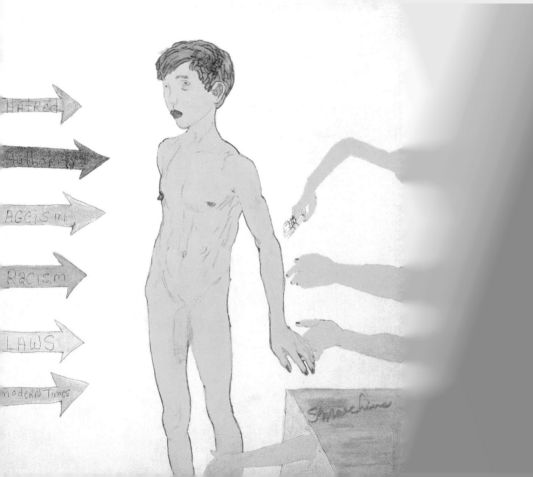

SAL MERCHINO
(c. 1955–)
Chicago
● *Ageism*
c. 1975
opaque watercolor on vinyl
12 × 10 ³/₄"
Gasperi Gallery, New Orleans

(oppsite) A self-taught painter
known for his sensual, homoerotic depiction of nude young
men, Sal Merchino is also dedicated to addressing social injus-
tice. This work explores the
plight of the young male hustler, trapped by a greedy and
uncaring society. Center stage is
a lithe youth, harassed and
boxed in by social forces that
are expressed allegorically by
Merchino as (on the right)
groping, money-proffering
hands, and (on the left) arrows
bearing the labels: HATRED,
AUTHORITY, AGEISM, RACISM, LAWS,
MODERN TIMES.

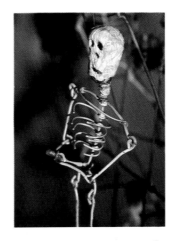

WAYNE McCAFFERY
(1923–1993)
Akron, Ohio
● *Skeleton Whirligig*
c. 1970
painted metal
57 × 37 × 18"
Collection of
Herbert Waide Hemphill, Jr.

This astounding whirligig
updates the Renaissance image
of the memento mori, or
reminder of the inevitability
of death. The jangling skele-
tons bear a message for the
imprudent. Set in motion by a
propeller, these bony figures
begin to greedily stroke their
horrifyingly red penises.
Despite the obvious humor,
this construction reads as a
profound warning against
the evils of onanistic indul-
gence in particular, and sexual
desire in general.

RALPH BUCKWALTER
Lancaster County, Pennsylvania
(1906–1990)
• *Bathing Beauty Cane*
c. 1970s
polychromed maple, and birch
35 × 9 ¾ × 1 ¾"
Collection of
Herbert Waide Hemphill, Jr.

This artist has reinvented the
pop-cultural feminine ideal of
his time—the bathing beauty—
in the highly personal genre of
cane carving. Wearing nothing
but a bathing suit and a pair of
shoes, this curvaceous bather
provides a sensual alternative
to the standard cane handle.
The structure of the cane
demands she be positioned—
awkwardly to be sure—on her
side, a passive counterpoint to
the comparatively masculine
activity of cane-carrying.

DENZIL GOODPASTER
(1908–)
• *Dolly Parton Cane*
1970s
polychromed wood and wire
32 ¾ × 2 ¼ × 7 ⅛"
Collection of
Herbert Waide Hemphill, Jr.

Dolly Parton, country music
diva and actress, has long been
America's favorite buxom
blonde; the size of her breasts
have been a consistent topic for
national debate. In this rather
wooden rendering of Dolly, her
famous anatomical attributes
have been emphasized.
Shown clutching a microphone,
the singer stares into space,
her bust and backside swelled
to mythical proportions.
This cane, like the bathing
beauty reproduced above, is
evidence of the pervasive
effect of mass media upon
traditional genres of folk art in
the twentieth century.

DWIGHT MACKINTOSH
(1906–)
California
• *Four Boys with
Brown and Tan Spots*
1980
ink and tempera
18 ¾ × 25 ¾"
The Ames Gallery,
Berkeley, California

• *Three Boys (One Seated)*
c. 1980
pencil and tempera
23 ½ × 35"
The Ames Gallery,
Berkeley, California

(opposite) Born in California,
Dwight Mackintosh was institutionalized for being "unman-
ageable at home" by age sixteen. He was to remain institutionalized until his release in
1978. Mackintosh was released
into the care of his brother,
who, remembering Dwight's
boyhood interest in art, took
him to The Creative Growth
Center in Oakland, California,
where he was provided with
the encouragement and materials to begin making art.
Mackintosh often portrays boys
in unconventional ways: Aside
from sporting huge, missilelike
erections, they are endowed
with voluptuous, feminine
breasts, bellies, and backsides.
One work features a group of
four boys, accompanied by a
stream-of-consciousness river of
barely readable text. In another,
three boys march toward an
unknown destination.

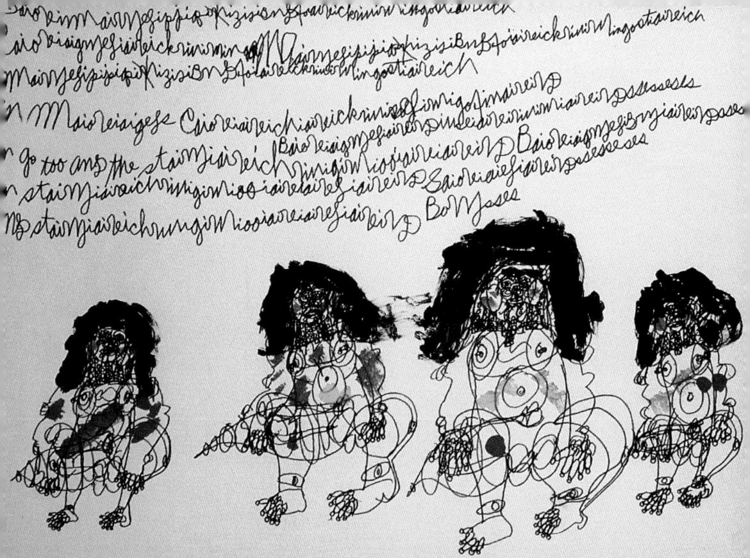

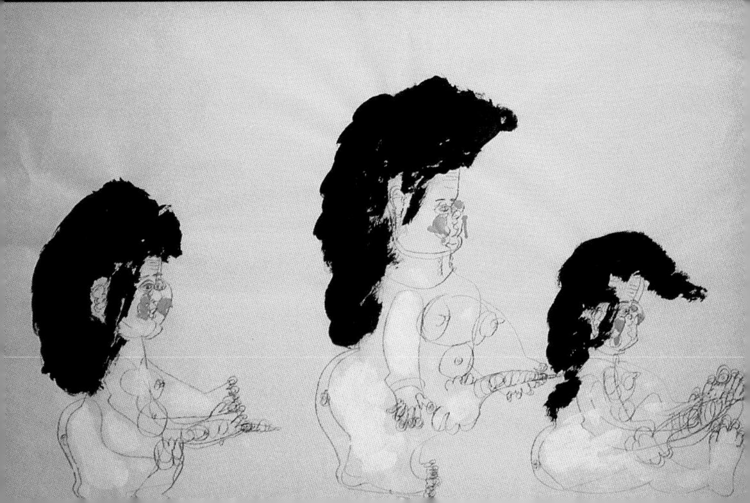

EDGAR TOLSON
(1904–1984)
Compton, Kentucky
*Adam and Eve
(The Original Sin)*
1975
wood
12 1/4 × 5 1/4 × 5 1/4"
Collection of
Herbert Waide Hemphill, Jr.

Adam and Eve
c. 1970s
polychromed wood
10 × 10 1/2 × 7 1/4"
National Museum of American
Art, Smithsonian Institution,
Washington, D.C. Gift of
Herbert Waide Hemphill, Jr.
(museum purchase made possible by Ralph Cross Johnson)

(opposite and top right) A native
Kentuckian, Edgar Tolson was a
young man when he became a
preacher. He served as a Baptist
pastor for many years before
retiring in 1961. Although
Tolson had been an intermittent
whittler during his life, the
beginning of his serious carving
oeuvre has been dated to
1957. Over the years, Tolson
carved about 100 works, often
addressing biblical themes.
(opposite) This carving is
Tolson's poignant rendering of
the moment of Original Sin.
Adam and Eve stand facing
each other, locked in the act of
intercourse, which is made all
the more intimate for their tender, heartfelt kiss. Their
embrace doesn't appear to be
sinful at all. A bit more racy is
another tableau *(top right)*, in
which the Garden of Eden is
the scene of decidedly ungodly
activities. Adam bends Eve
over the Tree, penetrating her
from behind, while the serpent
bites her breast.

WILLIAM EDMONSON
(c. 1865–1951)
Tennessee
Adam and Eve (and the Snake)
limestone
13 × 30 × 12"
The Marvill Collection

The African American carver
William Edmonson, born and
raised in Tennessee, was a
laborer for most of his life,
working on the railroad,
and later as a custodian at a
hospital. A man of visions,
Edmonson believed he was told
by God to become a stone
carver. Following divine
instructions, he began carving
memorials and tombstones,
subsequently turning to figural
works. Inspired by religion,
popular culture, and everyday
life, Edmonson's carvings are
deceptively simple and often
deliver penetrating psychological insights into his subjects.
This particular work takes a
sympathetic view of the plight
of Adam and Eve. They appear
seated, and instead of busying
themselves with Original Sin,
they look forlorn, withdrawn,
and vulnerable in the presence
of the giant snake.

WALTER REINSCH
Jamestown, New York
(1897–)

Cupid and Psyche: Seascape
c. 1970s
oil on board
16 1/2 × 24 1/4″
Jamison/Thomas Gallery,
Portland, Oregon

*The Modern Inferno: Ten Steps
to Hell, nos. 5 and 10*
c. 1940 –1960
paint on paper
17 × 11 1/2″
8 3/4 × 13″
Collection of
Linda and Gene Kangas

(top right) Walter Reinsch was
born in Kenmore, New York. A
self-taught painter of erotica,
Reinsch has added a new twist
to the myth of Cupid and
Psyche. In the mythology,
Cupid was the divine lover of
the beautiful mortal woman,
but here, Reinsch has portrayed
them both as star-crossed
angels. Weightless, they engage
in sexual acrobatics, each pre-
occupied with pleasuring the
other. What might have been
rendered as mere mortal erotica
in the hands of another artist
has been elevated to the lofty
and venerated genre of the
loves of the gods.
(bottom left and right) Less
pleasant is Reinsch's disturbing-
ly moralistic *Ten Steps to Hell*, a
series recounting what the artist
has imagined to be the ultimate
fate of sexual sinners. *(left)* This
composition features a crowd
of departed souls headed for
hell—ignorant of their destination, they continue to flirt and
copulate with each other.
(right) In another tableau,
Reinsch has imagined what
awaits women guilty of teasing
men during their lives. One has
been chained to a gigantic, vertical penis erupting like a vol-
cano, while two others are
mired in a sea of sperm. The
mind boggles at the
Hieronymus Bosch–like imagination responsible for such
vivid spectacles.

GUSTAVE KLUMPP
(1902–1980)
New York
*Dream of a Nudist Camp
Wedding*
1971
oil on canvas
24 × 30″
National Museum of American
Art, Smithsonian Institution,
Washington, D.C. Gift of
Herbert Waide Hemphill, Jr.
(museum purchase made possi-
ble by Ralph Cross Johnson)

Born in Germany, Gustave
Klumpp immigrated to New
York City in 1923. Trained in
his native land to work as a
compositor in a printing factory, he soon found work in
the printing industry in New
York, continuing in a career
that spanned forty years. Soon
after his retirement, Klumpp
began painting canvases that
often featured the female nude
or nude people in fantastical
settings. One example of what
he called his "fantasies," this
painting provides a forbidden
glimpse into an Eden-like nudist colony, in which nude couples romp on a tennis court or
recline on a blanket; a nudist
wedding is but one vignette
among many. Nude, carefree
children are also shown at play.
(See page 56 for a detail.)

ARTIST UNKNOWN
Cart
c. 1980
wood and enamel
10 × 9 × 5″
The Kinsey Institute for
Research in Sex, Gender
and Reproduction,
Bloomington, Indiana

Although somewhat primitive in
construction, this pull cart is
both sexy and entertaining. Like
most novelties, its charm is not
fully realized until it is set into
motion. The gimmick here is
simple—by pulling the cart, the
couple begins to copulate—and
while their intercourse has been
rendered quite awkward and
even brutish, it is nevertheless
frankly appealing.

ARTIST UNKNOWN
"Pecker" Fish Lures
c. 1980
polychromed basswood
3 1/4″
Hamilton Gallery,
Rumson, New Jersey

These small gems of erotica add
a bit of humor to the male-
dominated sport of fishing.
Although simple in conception,
these cottage industry "lures"
enact a sophisticated double
entendre. The penis is revealed
to be a barbed, dangerous, and
even potentially fatal hunting
weapon, but when one imagines the lures in use, the penis
becomes the fleeing prey.

HAROLD W. GEESAMAN
(1924–1988)
Dauthin County, Pennsylvania
Group of Women in Lake
1980
oil on canvas board
22 × 28″
Collection of Instinctuals,
Alexandria, Virginia

*The Great Sacrifice
(Ladies Club)*
1983
oil on panel
24 × 18″
Collection of Instinctuals,
Alexandria, Virginia

(opposite, top) Once a sign
painter in his native Pennsylvania, Harold Geesaman was
also a master of an eerie but
alluring brand of erotica.
Rendered in hallucinatory
detail, this composition is
overpopulated with latter-day,
post–sexual revolution bathing
beauties. All of a similar type,
these lithe, young nudes frolic
languorously in an idyllic
forest lake. The woman in
the foreground invites the
viewer to enter into the artist's
fantasy by seductively disrob-
ing, while the other members
of this erotic army seem to pas-
sively await the viewer's gaze.
(opposite, bottom) Another very
different painting by the same
artist provides a look into the
world of the drag queen. A fas-
cinated crowd looks on as a
muscular drag queen disrobes
upon a table while his lover,
looks on, at the lower left of
the composition. The artist has
manipulated the composition
to draw the viewer in as a
spectator to this scene, which
is shot through—as is reflected
in the grimaces of the seedy
audience members—with a
dose of the bizarre.

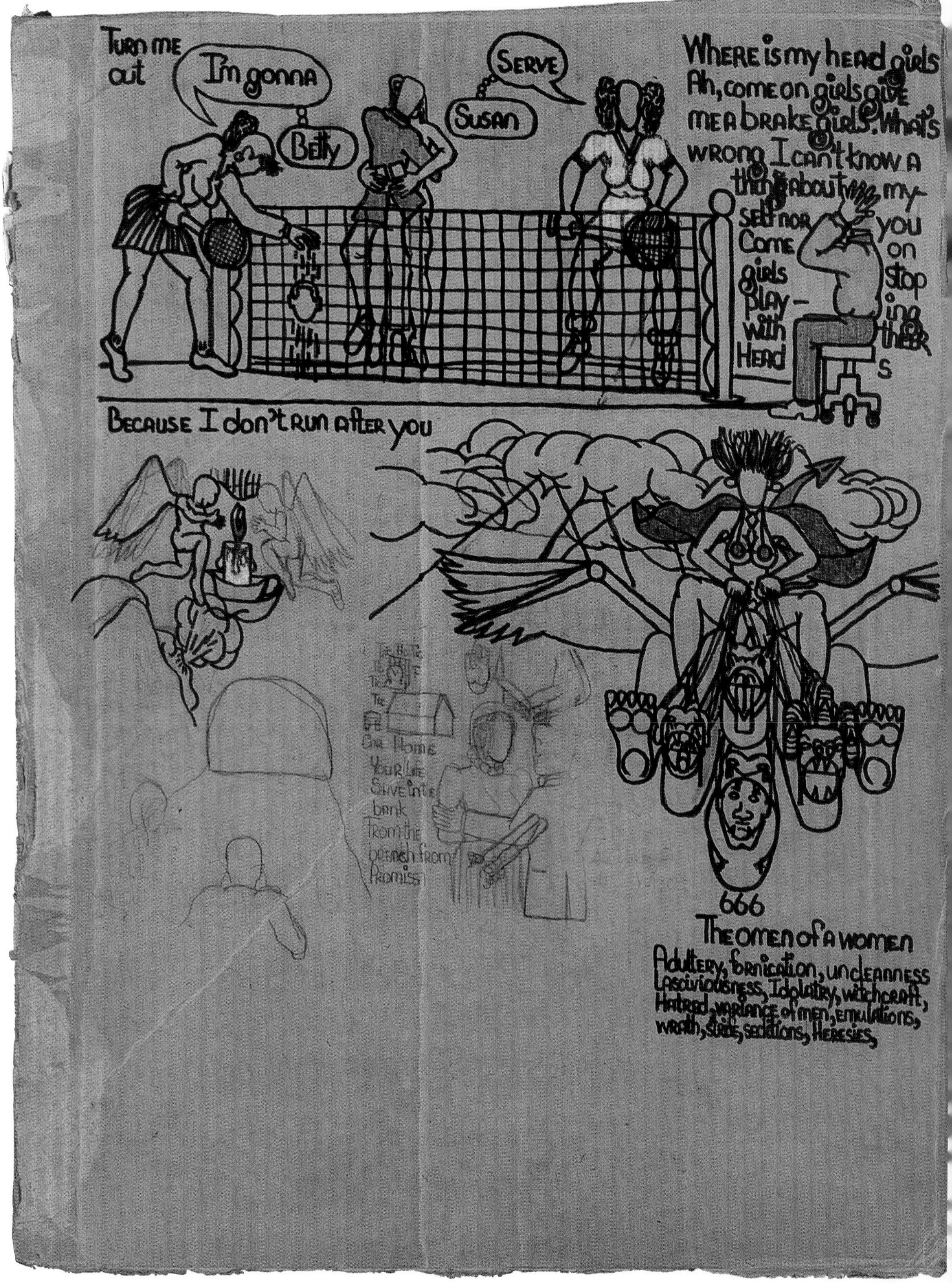
Turn me out
I'm gonna
Betty
Serve
Susan
Where is my head girls Ah, come on girls give me a brake girls. What's wrong I can't know a thing about my self nor you
Come girls play-with Head
on stop ing thier s
Because I don't run after you
Tic Tic Tic
Tic
Car Home
Your Life
Save in the bank
From the breach from Promiss
666
The omen of a women
Adultery, fornication, uncleanness Lasciviousness, Idolatry, witchcraft, Hatred, variance of men, emulations, wrath, strife, seditions, Heresies,

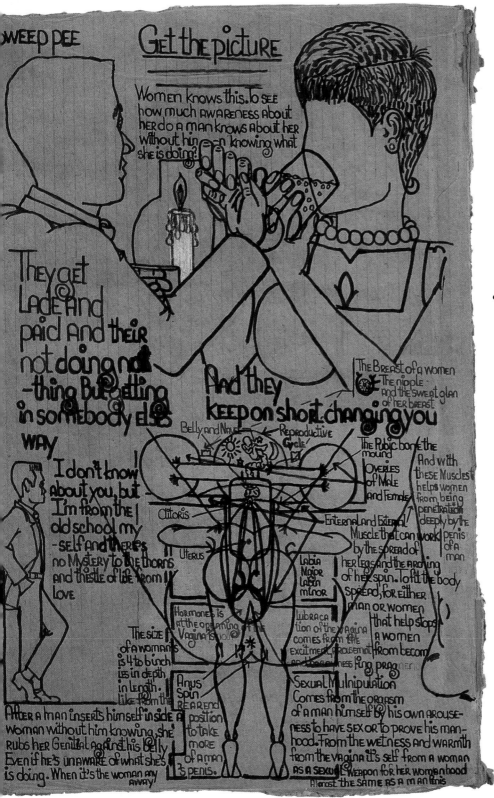

ARTIST UNKNOWN
● *Get the Picture*
c. 1980
crayon and felt marker on corrugated cardboard
23 × 31 ½″
Collection of Instinctuals, Alexandria, Virginia

This annotated ensemble of drawings goes right to the heart of the battle between the sexes. Clearly made by a man who was trying his best to understand the opposite sex, it provides us with a rare insight into the confusion that accompanies sexual desire. A series of scenarios relates, in a unique fashion, the vicissitudes of male sexual frustration. At the upper left, the artist has created a clever metaphor for the notion of head games, and at the upper right, the foibles of dating are laid bare. Elsewhere, a rather pessimistic view of the female gender is put across: In the center a faceless, all-powerful woman rides an imaginary beast, and to the lower right, the female nude is dissected in a bizarre, dadaist diagram. The artist summarizes his take on women with the following angry slogan: "They get lade and paid and their [sic] not doing nothing but getting in somebody else's way."

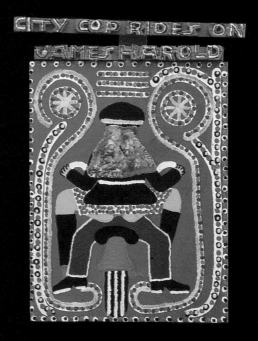

JAMES HAROLD JENNINGS
(1931–)
North Carolina
City Cop Rides On
c. 1980
polychromed wood
13 × 17″
Epstein/Powell Gallery,
New York

Man Gits Sat On
c. 1985
polychromed wood
8 1/2 × 19 1/4 × 2 1/2″
The Ames Gallery,
Berkeley, California

(opposite, top and bottom) Born
in Pinnacle, North Carolina
(near Winston-Salem), James
Harold Jennings worked odd
jobs such as night watchman
and (adult) film projectionist,
before suffering something of a
nervous breakdown in 1968.
When his mother died in 1974,
he inherited the family farm, at
which time he embarked upon
his work as an artist. Jennings
makes a variety of sculptural
objects out of wood, such as
whirligigs and relief plaques,
which he paints in bright
colors. Inspired by his eclectic
religious and philosophical
views, these works often contain sexual material, and he has
become famous for his dominant, buxom "Amazon" girls.
(opposite, top) In this work,
Jennings has cleverly
satirized the habits of city
policemen—while the cop
rides his motorcycle forward,
a woman "rides" the cop.
(opposite bottom) Another
work features one of the artist's
notorious Amazon dominatrix-
es, typically overpowering
a helpless man who lies on
the ground.

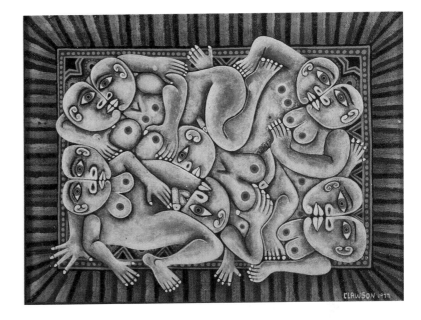

REX CLAWSON
(1933–)
Orgy
1977
oil on masonite
13 × 16 1/2″
Gasperi Gallery, New Orleans

It is not clear where one figure
begins and the other one ends
in this orgy scene. Rex
Clawson's imaginative figures
interact to create a composition
that is lively indeed. Round
heads echo round pairs
of breasts and testicles, and it
seems as if all the figures
are connected to the same
communal mass of flesh in one
way or another.

HENRY SPELLER
(1900–)
Memphis, Tennessee
*Man in Jumpsuit with Two
Standing Women*
c. 1980
graphite and crayon on paper
18 × 24″
Gasperi Gallery, New Orleans

(*opposite, top*) Born to a family of poor, African American share-croppers in Mississippi, Henry Speller eventually moved to Memphis, Tennessee, where he held a number of jobs, and began making the drawings he has become widely respected for. Speller, like his late wife, Georgia, is a purveyor of a lively and often sexually explicit figuration: His compositions are populated by explicit figures he calls "characters from Dallas." Yet the star of this work may very well be someone closer to Speller's home—the King himself. An elaborately bouffanted celebrity type, possibly Elvis, stands grinning at the center, flanked on either side by two long-legged groupies. Although they are fully dressed, the genitals of all three are exposed, suggesting the activity they plan to engage in. Here, Speller has captured the essence of America's rock 'n' roll fantasy.

GEORGIA SPELLER
(1931–1987)
Memphis, Tennessee
Orgy
c. 1980–1985
tempera on paper
18 × 24″
Collection of Robert Cargo Folk
Art Gallery, Tuscaloosa, Alabama

(*opposite, bottom*) The second wife of Henry Speller, Georgia Speller has become recognized as an artist in her own right. In this work, she has depicted a bizarre orgy. Figures of all shapes and sizes are shown engaged in a variety of sex acts; the composition is united by Speller's fluid line. The scale of the figures is wildly uneven, a note of formal chaos that rings throughout this fantastical scenario.

JIMMIE LEE SUDDUTH
(1910–)
Alabama
Man and Woman
1986
earth pigments, vegetable dyes, and housepaint on plywood panel
25 × 25″
Collection of Robert Cargo Folk Art Gallery, Tuscaloosa, Alabama

A denizen of the rural South, the African American, self-taught painter Jimmie Lee Sudduth worked as a laborer in a racially segregated world in which he has, nevertheless, in later years, earned recognition for his artistic achievements. An accomplished blues musician, Sudduth has become known for his unique method of painting, which involves using unconventional materials such as rock pigment, mud, sugar water, and berry juice. His works depict the people, animals, and architecture that comprise his hometown of Fayette, Alabama. This painting fancifully pictures a rather staged sexual encounter. A man and woman face forward—he takes charge, stimulating himself and his lover at the same time in what seems to be a blatantly exhibitionist romp.

JOHN SCHREINER
● *Orgy*
1978
acrylic on masonite
20 × 24″
Collection of Instinctuals,
Alexandria, Virginia

● *Female with Aura Holding Penis*
c. 1970
metal relief
12 × 9″
Collection of Instinctuals,
Alexandria, Virginia

In Schreiner's chaotic painting *(opposite, top)*, form follows content in an unprecedented orgiastic fantasy illuminating the lure that lesbian sexual activities hold for men. Although the figures have been rendered with some degree of realism, any sense of rational perspective has been subsumed by eruptions of Dionysian desire. Idealized women are shown engaged in a variety of erotic couplings and groups in quite graphic detail, and although no men appear, a variety of dildos serve as phallic stand-ins. Everything about this painting— the various poses, attitudes, and types of women involved— betray this scene as conceived to titillate male desire.

(opposite bottom) This relief is a slightly different excursion into the fantastic. A woman is rendered with exaggerated proportions—not only in her breast size, but in the size of the male organ she appears to possess. In Schreiner's universe, anything goes.

ULYSSES S. DAVIS
(1913–1992)
Savannah, Georgia
● *Where Life Comes From*
late 1970s–early 1980s
mahogany
11 1/2 × 5″
Collection of James E. Allen

Although the talented African American carver Ulysses S. Davis is best known for his portrait busts of American presidents, his work includes religious and various other subjects, including forays into erotica. A laborer in Georgia, when Davis retired, he set up the Ulysses Barber Shop, which he decorated with carvings and where he cut hair. This carving reveals a little-known side to Davis's work, but one that is entirely compatible with themes addressed in local barbershop chatter. Ulysses's formal wit is formidable—here he has carved a male figure that doubles as a penis, which, when turned around, changes once again, this time into a female figure.

ARTIST UNKNOWN
New York City
• *Graffiti*
c. 1970
spray paint on subway car

ARTIST UNKNOWN
New York City
• *Graffiti*
c. 1970
spray paint on Dumpster

ARTIST UNKNOWN
New York City
• *Graffiti*
1980
spray paint on brick wall

The art of graffiti is not recognized by many to be an art form at all but rather an urban nuisance. Although the phenomenon of decorating (or desecrating) city walls is an old one, it became especially popular during the seventies in New York City, and by the eighties, graffiti was transported from the streets to the galleries to become the latest rage in SoHo. A creative outlet for the dispossessed, often minority youth, graffiti became the raison d'être of young rebels who "bombed," or spray-painted, subway cars and just about every other surface imaginable with images and their "tags," or proud graffiti signatures. A contest of artistic skill, bravery, and machismo, graffiti—usually an extremely dangerous enterprise considering that it is illegal—often reflects a bombastic sexuality wielded as a language of power.

(top) Martha Cooper, a photographer of urban vernacular culture, has captured this work of by-now destroyed subway graffiti. An unknown artist has, with a few lines and minimal shading, created the rather buxom girl of his dreams. *(bottom)* A Dumpster became a canvas for another artist, who has transformed the male and female organs into quasireligious icons. *(opposite)* Another image, painted on the side of a building, illustrates a street-smart double entendre of power and sexual prowess that typifies graffiti turf battles. A huge, shaking vibrator is shown in the act of defeating his rival artists, or "Stompin' Out Toy Pussies." These three examples make explicit the libido that has always supercharged the art of graffiti.

ROGER RICE
(1958–)
● *Adam and Eve*
c. 1989
oil on old wood panel
38 × 32"
Collection of Robert Cargo
Folk Art Gallery,
Tuscaloosa, Alabama

This version of original sin is as unconventional as it is exciting. Formally activated by dramatic diagonals, the figures of Adam and Eve are lithe and powerfully animated. As Eve reaches across to pick the forbidden fruit, Adam moves to stop her, and warn her of the presence of the serpent. This painting is unique, not only in the artist's dramatic portrayal of the subject, which has historically been portrayed in a more subdued fashion, but also in his choice to represent this couple as black.

DAVID BUTLER
(1898–)
Louisiana
● *Erect Man*
1985
enamel on tin
25 × 25"
Gasperi Gallery, New Orleans

(opposite) Born in Good Hope, Louisiana, David Butler was instructed by God to make artwork that would transform his modest house and yard into an art environment, which has since, unfortunately, been destroyed. Butler, an African American, used tin roofing panels as his material: After flattening and cutting out shapes from the tin, he would paint them with bright colors, bringing to life the many human, animal, and mythical figures that came to populate his immediate world. As in most of his work, this figure is enlivened by a whimsical sense of humor. A bizarre, silhouetted figure stands with an erect penis, nearly as large as the figure itself, which points skyward like an arrow. Although Butler is not known exclusively for erotica, this work is an entertaining contribution.

132

133

ROYAL ROBERTSON
(1936–)
Baldwin, Louisiana
Now the Vision Dreams
c. 1990
mixed media on posterboard
28 × 22"
Collection of Robert Cargo
Folk Art Gallery,
Tuscaloosa, Alabama

(opposite) Inspired by a marriage gone bad, the African American visionary artist Royal Robertson built an identity—"Prophet" Royal Robertson—and an art environment in and around his home (all of which was destroyed in a hurriane), dedicated to reviling and protecting himself against "whores" and female "vipers." A schizophrenic, Robertson imagines himself to have been the victim of a grand plot driven by feminine evil, and many of his works reflect this belief. This drawing ferociously documents his experience and what he perceives to be the evils of women, with both images and Scripture-like text. Beneath the anger, one detects a lingering fascination for the erotic.

JOSEPH HARDIN
(1921–1989)
Birmingham, Alabama
Woman Abducting Man
c. 1975
mixed media on paper
17 × 14"
Collection of Robert Cargo
Folk Art Gallery,
Tuscaloosa, Alabama

Plagued by the rheumatoid arthritis that crippled him, Joseph Hardin drew and painted to escape his pain and express himself. His works often envision sexual fantasies populated by outrageous figures, and his style unselfconsciously evokes a variety of modernist visual strategies. In this work, the artist has imagined an erotic scenario in which an otherworldly nude woman carries off her male victim, who appears to welcome his abduction.

IVAN LAYCOCK
(1930–)
Michigan
● *Birdhouse*
1990
tin, wood, beads, rope hair, sta-
ples, dowels, masonite, spray
paint, stencil, and wire hanger
17 × 17 1/2 × 10 1/4″
Collection of Jim Linderman

Ivan Laycock is a retired auto
worker from Michigan who cur-
rently lives with his mail-order
bride, and who creates mixed
media artworks such as
whirligigs and birdhouses. To
build this birdhouse, Laycock
has used a variety of media to
transform an everyday object
into an impressive sculpture in
the round. The roof of this
birdhouse is decorated by
phallic forms, and the walls
bear anatomically explicit
figures—to the right, male and
female figures seem poised on
the brink of copulation, and to
the left, a buxom female figure
emerges in relief. One wonders
if any birds would dare to
visit such an outrageously decorated birdhouse.

136

WALTER TITER
Wisconsin
● *Two Pigs*
1981
wood
3 1/8 × 6 1/4 × 2 1/4″
Collection of
Herbert Waide Hemphill, Jr.

(right) This tiny handheld
erotic toy is basic but quite
amusing. Two carved pigs
stand in their instinctual mating
position, and when activated
with a simple mechanism,
nature takes its course.

ARTIST UNKNOWN
Chicago
● *Bra (Prison Art)*
1980s
folded cigarette wrappers
4 1/4 × 13 3/4 × 13″
American Primitive Gallery,
New York

(opposite) Created according
to the make-do theory of
aesthetics, this homemade bras-
sière is a testimony to this
prison inmate's ingenuity.
Fashioned by folding and linking together many cigarette
packages, it approximates the
voluptuous proportions of a
fantasy woman. Visually
enlivened by the play of
different cigarette logos, this
artwork improves upon the
mundane article of clothing
that inspired it.

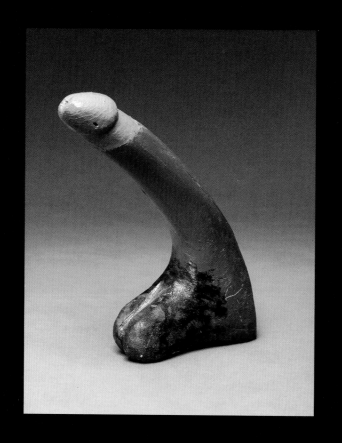

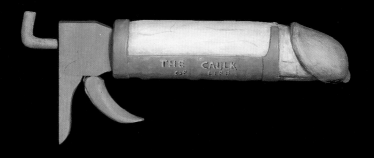

JEFF WILLIAMS
(1958–)
North Carolina
Carved Penis
May 1989
oak
9 1/4 × 3 × 5 3/4″
Collection of Helen Marden

(opposite, top) A devout
Christian, the talented African
American carver Jeff Williams
turned his attention to making
art in 1982 as a creative outlet
and to offset negative influ-
ences in his life. His carvings
are marked by an extremely
graceful figuration, which has
extended to this rendering of a
particular piece of male anatomy. Complete with a set of real-
istically shaped testicles, this
penis stands relatively
erect, its shape outlining a
pleasant arc.

JACK McILNAY
(1934–)
Alexandria, Virginia
Caulk of Life
1991
wood
3 1/4 × 1 1/2 × 9″
Collection of Charles G. Haak

(opposite, bottom) This carved
object is a masterpiece of
sexual punnery. The artist has
reinvented the familiar shape
of a caulking gun, adding a
penis shape where the nozzle
would have been, and when
the trigger is pulled, a white
substance is emitted, comically
simulating orgasm. This work
cleverly equates male sexual
performance with that of a
mundane tool.

139

JOEL LAGE
(1939-)
New Mexico
Cowboy Blow-Job
1992
tin cans, bottle caps, wire, and
paint
10 3/8 × 9 × 4″
Leslie Muth Gallery, Sante Fe

Born in Charles City, Iowa, Joel
Lage moved west (Oregon,
California, and New Mexico) in
the 1960s. A resident of north-
ern New Mexico since 1982,
Lage creates artwork from cast-
off objects and materials—especially tin cans. This particular
assemblage provides a glimpse

of the Wild West that never
quite made it into the movies. A
rare depiction of a homosexual
encounter between two cow-
boys, this ensemble is inscribed
by an amusing narrative on the
back of the kneeling figure,
which reads: "July 14, 1882.
In a secluded arroyo outside
Prescott, Arizona, Oyster Tex
blows the Yellow Kid." Any
potential threat that this scene
might deliver to the manly
(heterosexual) myth of the
cowboy is defused with a near-
slapstick humor. *(See page 57*
for detail.)

SULTAN ROGERS
(1922–)
Syracuse, New York
Oral Sex
Mid 20th century
pine
12 1/2 × 3 1/2″
Collection of
Albert and Jane Hunecke

Born near Oxford, Mississippi,
Sultan Rogers learned the trade
of carpentry from his father, a
skill that gave him the freedom
to travel north and ultimately
settle in Syracuse, New York.
His facility for carving wood
was apparent early on, and
eventually his painted carvings
in soft wood of people, animals, and even vampires came
to the attention of the noted
Mississippi folklorist William
Ferris. An important part of
Rogers's creative process is his
attention to dreams of what he
calls "futures"—vivid images of
works that he executes upon
waking. The erotic component
of his oeuvre is quite evident in
this carving of a couple strenu-
ously engaged in oral sex.
Here, Rogers has imaginatively
transformed a common sexual
theme into an impressive dis-
play of bedroom acrobatics, in
which gravity holds no sway
over sexual desire.

ARTIST UNKNOWN
Indiana
Stroh's (Beer Can Man)
20th century
beer can, tabs, bottle caps, and
mixed media
10 1/2 × 4 1/2 × 3 1/2″ (closed)
13 1/2 × 4 1/2 × 3 1/2″ (open)
Private Collection

(opposite) These "before" *(left)*
and "after" *(right)* shots illustrate the workings of a simple
but surprisingly effective erotic
novelty, likely a modern variation on the venerable "barrel-
man" genre. The artist has cleverly recycled garbage into a
very entertaining toy. At rest,
the figure does not appear to
harbor any secrets, but by rais-
ing the can, one causes the
effect of dropped trousers,
revealing this figure's previously
hidden erection.

Andrews, Ruth, ed.
How to Know American Folk Art.
New York: E.P. Dutton, 1977.

Aratow, Paul. *100 Years of Erotica:
A Photographic Portfolio of
Mainstrean American Subculture
from 1845–1945.* San Francisco:
Straight Arrow Books, 1973.

Barnes, F.A. *Canyon Country
Prehistoric Rock Art.*
Salt Lake City, Utah:
Wasatch Publishers, 1989.

Baynes, Ken. *Art in Society.*
Woodstock, N.Y.: The Overlook
Press, 1975.

Becker, Claus, et al.
Museum der Erotischen Kunst.
Munich, Germany: Heyne, 1992.

Boullet, Jean. *Symbolisme Sexuel.*
Paris: J.J. Pauvert, 1961.

Bourgeron, Jean-Pierre. *Les
Masques d' Eros.* Paris:
Les Editions de l'Amateur, 1985.

Bowie, Theodore, et al.
Studies in Erotic Art.
New York: Basic Books, 1970.

Brown, Milton W., et al.
*American Art: Painting, Sculpture,
Architecture, Decorative Arts,
Photography.*
New York: Harry N. Abrams, 1979.

Cardinal, Roger. *Ousider Art.*
London: StudioVista, 1972.

Cooper, Martha, and Henry
Chalfant. *Subway Art.*
New York: Henry Holt, 1984.

D'Emilio, John, and Estelle B.
Freedman. *Intimate Matters: A
History of Sexuality in America.*
New York: Harper and Row, 1988.

Dissanayake, Ellen. *The Depiction
of Sexuality in Art: From Premodern
Awe to Postmodern Ennui.*
Article in *The World & I.* a publica-
tion of the *Washington Times,*
January 1993.

Doig, Federico Kauffman.
Sexual Behaviour in Ancient Peru.
Lima, Peru: Kompaktos, 1979.

Douglas, Nik, and Penny Slinger.
*The Pillow Book: The Erotic
Sentiment and the Paintings of
India, Nepal, China, & Japan.*
New York: Arlington House, 1981.

Ellis, Kate , et al. *Caught Looking:
Feminism, Pornography &
Censorship.*
East Haven, Conn.: Long River
Books, 1992.

Evans, Tom, and Mary Anne Evans.
Shunga: The Art of Love in Japan.
London: Paddington Press, 1975.

Ewers, John C. *Plains Indian
Sculpture: A Traditional Art from
America's Heartland.*
Washington, D.C: Smithsonian
Institution Press, 1986.

Feest, Christian F. *Native Arts of
North America.* London: Thames
and Hudson, 1980 and 1992.

Ginzburg, Ralph. *An Unhurried
View of Erotica.* New York:
The Helmsman Press, 1958.

Grosbois, Charles.
Shunga: Images of Spring.
Geneva, Switzerland: Nagel, 1964.

Guthman, William H. *Drums A'beat-
ing Trumpets Sounding: Artistically
Carved Powder Horns in the
Provincial Manner 1746–1781.*
Hartford, Conn.: The Connecticut
Historical Society, 1993.

Hardy, D.E. *Eye Tattooed America.*
Honolulu: Hardy Marks
Publications, 1993.

Hartigan, Lynda Roscoe. *Made with
Passion: The Hemphill Folk Art
Collection.* Washington, D.C:
Smithsonian Institution Press, 1990.

Hemphill, Herbert W., Jr., ed.
Folk Sculpture, USA.
Brooklyn, N.Y.:
Brooklyn Museum, 1976.

Hemphill, Herbert W., Jr., and Julia
Weissman. *Twentieth-Century
American Folk Art and Artists.*
New York: E.P. Dutton, 1974.

Hess, Thomas B. and Linda Nochlin,
ed. *Woman as Sex Object: Studies in
Erotic Art, 1730-1970.*
New York: *Newsweek,* 1972.

Holstein, Philip M., and Donnelley
Erdman. *Enduring Visions: 1,000
Years of Southwestern Indian Art.*
Aspen, Colo.: Aspen Center for the
Visual Arts, 1979.

Hornung, Clarence P. *Treasury of
American Design and Antiques.*
New York: Harry N. Abrams, 1972.

Jakovski, Anatole. *Éros du
Dimanche.*
Paris: J.J. Pauvert, 1964.

Kahmen, Volker. *Erotic Art Today.*
Greenwich, Conn.: New York
Graphic Society, 1971.

Kronhausen, Phyllis, and Eberhard
Kronhausen. *Erotic Art: A Survey
of Erotic Fact and Fancy in the
Fine Arts.*
New York: Bell Publishing, 1968.

——— *The Complete Book of
Erotic Art.*
New York: Bell Publishing, 1978.
(Orig vol. *Erotic Art.* New York:
Grove Press, 1968)

——— *The International Museum
of Erotic Art. Catalog.*
San Francisco: 1973.

Larco Hoyle, Rafael. *Checan: Essay
on Erotic Elements in Peruvian Art.*
Geneva, Switzerland: Nagel, 1965.

La Roche, Louanne. *Sam Doyle.*
Kyoto: Kyoto Shoin, 1989.

Legman, G. *Love & Death:
A Study in Censorship.*
New York: Breaking Point, 1949.

———. *The Horn Book: Studies in
Erotic Folklore and Bibliography.*
New Hyde Park, N.Y.: University
Books, 1964.

Livingston, Jane, and John
Beardsley. *Black Folk Art in
America: 1930–1980.*
Jackson, Miss.: University Press of
Mississippi and the Center for the
Study of Southern Culture, 1982.

Lo Duca, J.M. *A History of
Eroticism.* Paris: J.J. Pauvert, 1961.

Lucie-Smith, Edward. *Eroticism in
Western Art.* New York:
Praeger Publishers, 1972.

MacGregor, John.
*Dwight Mackintosh: The Boy Who
Time Forgot.*
San Francisco, Calif.: Creative
Growth Art Center, 1992.

Manley, Roger. *Signs and Wonders:
Outsider Art Inside North Carolina.*
Raleigh: North Carolina Museum
of Art, 1989

Naisse, Andy, and Maude Southwell
Wahlman. *Baking in the Sun:
Visionary Images from the South.*
Lafayette, La.: University Art
Museum of the University of
Southern Louisiana, 1987.

Patterson, Tom. *St. EOM in the
Land of Pasaquan: The Life and
Times of Eddie Owens Martin.*
N.C.: The Jargon Society, 1987.

Polley, Robert L,. ed. *America's Folk
Art: Treasures of American Folk Arts
and Crafts in Distinguished
Museums and Collections.*
Waukesha, Wis.: Country
Beautiful, 1971.

Rawson, Philip, ed.
Primitive Erotic Art.
New York: G.P. Putnam's
Sons, 1973.

Ricco, Roger, and Frank Maresca.
*American Primitive: Discoveries in
Folk Sculpture.*
New York: Alfred A. Knopf, 1988.

Romer, Grant B. *Die Erotische
Daguerreotype.*
Freiburg, Germany: Weingarten,
1990.

Rosenak, Chuck, and Jan Rosenak.
*Museum of American Folk Art
Encyclopedia of Twentieth-Century
American Folk Art and Artists.*
New York: Abbeville Press, 1990.

Rossi, William A. *The Sex Life of the
Foot and Shoe,.* rev. ed.
Hertfordshire, England: Wordsworth
Editions Ltd., 1977.

Schaafsma, Polly. *Indian Rock Art
of the Southwest.*
Santa Fe, N. Mex.: University of
New Mexico Press, 1980.

Smith Bradley. *Erotic Art of the
Masters: The 18th, 19th, and 20th
Centuries.*
Secaucus, N.J.: Lyle Stuart, 1974.

———. *The American Way of Sex: An
Informal Illustrated History.*
New York: Gemini Smith, 1978.

Szabo, George. *I Modi: The Sixteen
Pleasures — An Erotic Album of the
Italian Renaissance.*
Evanston, Ill.: Northwestern
University Press, 1988.

Tannahill, Reay. *Sex in History.*
New York: Stein and Day, 1980.

Thévoz, Michel. *Art Brut.*
New York: Rizzoli, 1976.

Thomas, P. *Kama Kalpa—The
Hindu Ritual of Love.*
Bombay, India: D.B. Taraporevala,
1960.

Thorn, Mark. *Taboo No More: The
Phallus in Fact, Fiction, and
Fantasy.*
New York: Shapolsky Publishers,
1990.

Valant, Gary M. *Vintage Aircraft
Nose Art.*
Osceola, Wis.: Motorbook
International, 1987.

142

Adam and Eve (Rice), 132
Adam and Eve (Tolson), 117
Adam and Eve (and the Snake) (Edmonson), 117
Adam and Eve (The Original Sin) (Tolson), 117
Advertising pieces, 54
African American artists, 94, 100, 103, 107, 108, 117, 126, 129, 132, 135, 139
African art, 9, 12
Ageism (Merchino), 113
AIDS, 59
Airplane nose paintings, 58, 80
Anal intercourse, 16, 32, 60, 72
Aprons, 75
Archie's Tavern (novelty), 94
Architectural edifices, imaginary, 59, 77
Articulated figures, 42, 43, 64, 84, 85, 92
Artist and Model (painting), 47
Ashby, Steven, 59, 110
Ashanti people, 9

Baby-boom era, 59
Ball-headed club, 21
Baroque period, 8, 13
Barrel people, 75
Bas-relief plaques, 34, 51
Bathing beauties, 58, 66, 70–71
cane, 114
Beardsley, Aubrey, 8, 13
Bellmer, Hans, 8
Bernini, Gian, 8, 13
Bestiality, 16, 51
Biblical imagery, 117, 132, 135
Bird Box (novelty), 66
Birdhouses, 7, 136
Birth of Venus (Hardin), 135
Book novelties, 31, 85
Bootjack, 53
Botticelli, Sandro, 71
Boucher, Francois, 13
Bound Witch (wood carving), 44
Bra, 136
Breast water bottle, 19
Buckwalter, Ralph, 114
Burlesque Show (Gatto), 99
Butler, David, 59, 132
Buzz Job (airplane nose art), 80

Calipers, 46
Canes, 27, 41, 114
Carpenter, Miles B., 59, 109
Carpenter's tool chest, 39
Carved Female Figure, 30
Carved Penis (Williams), 139
Catlin, George, 27
Ceramics, 7
    Native American, 9, 12–13, 16, 18, 19
    nineteenth-century, 28, 29
    pre-Columbian, 8
    sewer tile art, 42, 74
Cherokees, 60
Chimu people, 12
China, 9, 12
Cigar box assemblage, 78
Cigarette package bra, 136
Circus banner, 92

City Cop Rides On (Jennings), 125
Civil rights movements, 59
Classical revival, 26, 35, 48
Clawson, Rex, 125
Club, ball-headed, 21
Coffin art, 6, 39
Colonial America, 9, 12, 13
    powder horns, 22–23
    wood carving, 20
Comic strips, 104
Cooper, Martha, 130
Couple (bas-relief plaque), 51
Couple (Dubuffet), 9
Couple on a Table (bas-relief plaque), 34
Couple on Cart, 120
Courbet, Gustave, 9
Cowboy Blow-Job (Lage), 139
Cradle of Love (Mesisco), 99
Cuban Americans, 98
Cunnilingus, 104, 118, 139, 140
Cupid and Psyche: Seascape (Reinsch), 118

Daguerrotype, 51
Dakota, 32
David (Michelangelo), 9
Davis, Ulysses S., 129
D'Emilio, John, 26
Devil (Carpenter), 109
Dial, Thornton, Sr., 103
Dolly Parton Cane (Goodpaster), 114
Double Trouble (airplane nose art), 80
Doyle Sam, 59, 108
Drag queens, 121
Dream of a Nudist Camp Wedding (Klumpp), 119
Dubuffet, Jean, 9

Ecstasy of Saint Theresa, The (Bernini), 8
Edmonson, William, 117
Effigy pottery, 18
Effigy sticks, 27, 45
Ellis, Havelock, 58
Embroidery, 99
Environment (Visionary), 97
Erect Man (Butler), 132
Eskimo, 45
Evans, Minnie, 83
Examination of the Herald, The (Beardsley), 8
Expressionism, 8
Extramarital sex, 26, 58

Fabric art, 75, 99
Fajen, Henry, 71
Fast Company (airplane nose art), 80
Fellatio, 60, 118, 139, 140
    in Native American art, 19
Female Figure, 9, 20
Female Nude (McCarthy), 88
Female with Aura Holding Penis (Schreiner), 129
Feminists, 59
Ferris, William, 140
Fertility rituals, 15
Fetishism, 46
Figureheads, 26, 48

Fishing rods, 27, 48
Fish lures, 120
Flash, 87
Four Boys with Brown and Tan Spots (Mackintosh), 114
Fox Chase, The (Fajen), 71
Fragonard, Jean-Honoré, 9, 13
Freedman, Estelle B., 26
Free love, 26, 59
Fremont, 8, 15
French, Ichabod, 23
French and Indian War, 13, 22, 23
Freud, Sigmund, 46, 58
Funeral art, Native American, 18

Galatea, 48
Gatto, Victor Joseph, 99
Geesman, Harold W., 120
Gender identity, 26
Get the Picture, 123
Gichner, Lawrence Ernst, 6
Glassware, 7
    nineteenth-century, 28
Gleason, Herbert, 48
Golden Age, The (manuscript illumination), 9
Goodpaster, Denzil, 114
Graffiti, 7, 130
Great American Nude (Wesselmann), 9
Great Sacrifice, The (Ladies Club) (Geesman), 120
Greece, classical, 8, 13
Green Stockings (McCarthy), 88
Grosz, George, 8
Group of Women in Lake (Geesman), 120
Guns, 27
    toy, 72

Hale, Joe L., 39
Hand Hammer, 21
Hand toys, 72, 136
Happy Lovers, The (Fragonard), 9
Hardin, Joseph, 135
He/She (Doyle), 108
Hemphill, Herbert Wade, Jr., 7
Hermaphrodites, 98, 115
Hindu temple sculpture, 9, 12
Hirshfield, Morris, 59, 91
Hogarth, William, 13
Homosexuality, 27, 59, 72, 113, 120, 121, 139
    among African Americans, 108
    among Native Americans, 16, 27, 32, 33
    novelties depicting, 72
Hopi people, 97
Hunting rifles, 27

Ice Cream on Blue Monday (Rinaldi), 106
Ice fishing rod, 48
Illuminations, 9
Immigrants, 59
Incubus (Demon of Lust) (Rinaldi), 106
India, 9, 12
Indian clubs, 54
Industrialization, 26
Inseparable Friends (Hirshfield), 91
Ivory carving, 30
    See also Scrimshaw

Janis, Sidney, 91
Japan, 8, 12
Jeff on Top (Dirty) (Koons), 9

Jennings, James Harold, 59, 125
"Jiggle-sticks," 48
Jiggs (ceramic figure), 74
Jones, Louis C., 6

Kachina doll, 97
Kamasutra, 12
Kehoe, S. D., 54
Kitchen tools, 27, 30
Klumpp, Gustave, 59, 119
Koons, Jeff, 9, 59
Korean War, 58, 80
Kronhausen, Eberhard, 6
Kronhausen, Phyllis, 6

Lady with Fish (Dial), 103
Lage, Joel, 139
Laycock, Ivan, 136
Leda and the Swan (Rubens), 8
Legman, Gerson, 6
Lesbians, 59, 66, 91, 129
Lich, Rod, 7
Limberjack toy, 92
Lincoln, Abraham, 42
Love 1850 (scrimshaw), 36
Love manuals, Chinese, 9, 12
Loves of the Gods, The (Romano), 8

McCaffery, Wayne, 113
McCarthy, Justin, 59, 88
McIlainy, Jack, 139
Mackintosh, Dwight, 59, 114
Madam Queens Beauty Shoppe (novelty), 69
Man and Woman (Sudduth), 126
Man Exposed, 94
Man Gits Sat On (Jennings), 125
Man in a Barrel (wood carving), 74
Man in Jumpsuit with Two Standing Women (Speller), 126
Man with Guitar (Odio), 98
Manuscript illumination, 9
Martin, Eddie Owens (Saint EOM), 97
Masturbation, 49, 51, 54, 113
Matisse, Henri, 71
Memento mori, 113
Merchino, Sal, 113
Mesisco, George, 99
Michelangelo, 9, 13
Militaria, 7, 58
    colonial American, 13
    World War I, 60
    World War II, 58, 60, 80
    See also Weapons
Mimbres people, 9, 12–13, 16
Minor, Richardson, 22
Mirrors, 54
    Roman, 8
Miss Behavin' (airplane nose art), 80
Mississippian culture, 13, 18, 19
Miss Laid (airplane nose art), 80
Miss Moller (polychromed wood), 61
Modern Inferno, The: Ten Steps to Hell, nos. 5 and 10 (Reinsch), 118
Museum of Modern Art, 91

Native Americans, 12–21, 26–27, 44, 45, 97
    ceramics, 9, 12–13, 16–19
    petroglyphs, 8, 12-13, 15
    pipe bowls, 8, 27, 32, 60
    pre-Columbian, 8, 12, 14–19

Naughty Nellie (bootjack), 53
Near Miss (airplane nose art), 80
Novelties, 27, 39, 42, 58, 63, 74, 84,
    94, 120, 140,
Now the Vision Dreams
    (Robertson), 135
Nude (Savitsky), 100
Nude at the Window (Hirshfield), 91
Nude Carving, 88
Nude Couple (polychromed wood), 72
Nude Woman Cane, 41
Nude Woman Carving, 89
Nye, Henry Clay, 39

Oceania, 9, 12
Odio, Saturnion Portuondo "Pucho,"
    59, 98
Old Hag (Doyle), 108
Oral sex, 118, 139, 140
    See also Fellatio and Cunnilingus
Orgies, 45, 107, 118, 125, 126
    lesbian, 129
Origin of the World, The (Courbet), 9
Our Gal (airplane nose art), 80
"Outsiders," 59

Paddle, incised, 45
Paintings, 59
    nineteenth-century, 47
    on planes, 58
    See also specific works
Paleolithic era, 8, 13
Parrett, Susan, 7
Parton, Dolly, 114
Pasaquan (Saint EOM), 97
Pawnees, 8
"Peekaboo" pieces, 27
Penis Cane, 41
144 Performance art, 59
Petroglyphs, 8, 12–15
Photographs of Marie (Von
    Bruenchenhein), 82
Picasso, Pablo, 9
Pie crimper, 30
Pin-up girls, 58, 78
    in airplane nose art, 80
Pipe bowls, 8, 27, 32, 60
Plains Indians, 27, 60
Plaques, bas-relief, 34, 51
Pornography, 59
Portrait busts, 35
Pot holders, 75
Poupée, La (Bellmer), 8
Powder horns, 13, 22, 23
Pre-Columbian art, 9, 12, 14–19
Premarital sex, 26, 58
Presley, Elvis, 126
Pressley, Daniel, 100
Primal Glimse (Rizzoli), 77
Prison art, 6, 58, 84, 98, 104, 106, 139
Prostitution, 26, 108
    male, 113
Pueblo art, 12
Pull cart novelty, 120
Pygmalion, 48

Reclining Lady
    (polychromed pine), 78
Reclining Nude (relief carving), 68
Reinsch, Walter, 118
Religious right, 59
Renaissance, 8, 9, 13, 113
Rice, Roger, 132
Richard, Anton, and MoseT
    (Tolliver), 107
Rifles, 27, 53

Rinaldi, Michael, 106
Rizzoli, Achilles G., 59, 77
Robertson, Royal, 59, 135
Rockingham glaze, 29
Rococo period, 9, 13
Rogers, Sultan, 140
Romano, Giulio, 8, 13
Rome, ancient, 8
Rowlandson, Thomas, 8, 13
Rubens, Peter Paul, 8

Sack Time Sal II (airplane nose art), 80
Sailors' items, 6, 26
St. Clair, Leonard ("Stoney") L., 87
Savitsky, Jack, 100
Schizophrenia, 135
Schreiner, John, 129
Scrimshaw, 26, 36
September Morn, 64
Sewer tile art, 42, 74
Sexual Fantasy (Lady on a Scooter)
    (Tolliver), 9, 107
Sexual revolution, 59
Shannon, Charles, 94
Shell casings, 58, 60
Shoe fetish, 46
Shunga, 8, 12
Sign painting, 71
Silhouette sticks, 63
Sioux, 32, 45
Skeleton Whirligig (McCaffery), 113
Slave jugs, 28
Slightly Dangerous
    (airplane nose art), 80
Snuffboxes, 46
Soul Drane (Taylor), 104
Speller, Georgia, 59, 126
Speller, Henry, 59, 126
Spoon figures, 84–85
Sports pieces, 7, 27, 48
Stencils, 94
Stoneware jug, 28
Stroh's (Beer Can Man), 140
Sudduth, Jimmie Lee, 126
Summer Day Chore, A (Pressley), 100
Surrealism, 8

Tambling, Stephen, 22
Tao, 12
Tattoos, 7, 58
    flash, 87
Taylor, Richard, 104
Teapot, ceramic frog, 19
Temple sculpture, Hindu, 9, 12
Teton Sioux, 45
Three Boys (one seated)
    (Mackintosh), 114
Three Women on the Beach ("MH"), 71
Thumb Girl pieces, 54
Tin stencils, 94
Titer, Walter, 136
Tlingit people, 44
Tobacco cleavers, 46
Toby jugs, 29
Tolliver, Mose, 9, 59, 107
Tolson, Edgar, 59, 117
Tool chest, 39
Tools, 7
    kitchen, 27, 30
    Native American, 21
    workmen's, 27, 46, 139
Toothpick, 30
Toys, 6, 27, 92
    handheld, 72, 136
    See also Novelties
Traylor, Bill, 94

Trench art, 60
Trent, Robert F., 13
Two Pigs (Titer), 136
Two Women (wood carving), 66
Two Women with Tiger (Dial), 103

Urbanization, 26

Vase painting, classical Greek, 8
Venus (wood carving), 77
Venus of Willendorf, 8
Victory dance stick, 45
Von Bruenchenhein, Eugene, 59, 82
Voyeurism, 27, 51, 69, 91
Vulva, carved, 39

Watteau, Antoine, 13
Weapons
    Native American, 12, 21
    nineteenth-century, 53
    See also Militaria
Wesselmann, Tom, 9
Whalers, 26, 36
Where Life Comes From (Davis), 129
Whirligigs, 110, 113, 124, 136
Whoopy (Fajen), 71
Williams, Jeff, 139
Witches, 44
Woman (Evans), 83
Woman (Ashby), 110
Woman Abducting Man, 135
Woman and Centaur (Ashby), 110
Woman with an Ear of Corn
    (cast-iron plaque), 51
Woman with Fish (Dial), 102
Woman with Pig (bronze plaque), 51
Woodbridge Figures, 65
Wood carvings
    colonial American, 20
    Native American, 21, 44, 45
    nineteenth-century, 34, 39, 42
    twentieth-century, 60, 63, 64, 66,
    69–72, 74-75. 77, 88, 92, 98, 109,
    117, 129, 136, 139, 140
Workers
    off-hour creations by, 6–7, 42, 76
    tools used by, 27, 39
World War I, 58, 60
World War II, 58, 60
    airplane nose art, 80

Yankee Salute (tin cutout), 43
Ye Old Maide ("Marty"), 78
Yerrick, W., 66
Yost, Leon C., 15
Youth culture, 59

PHOTOGRAPHY CREDITS

The photographers and the sources of
photographic material other than those
indicated in the captions are as follows:

William Abranowicz, 54 *(bottom right)*, 55;

Gary Andrashko, 30 *(left)*, 39 *(top)*;

Joel Breger, 63, 79, 96, 100, 103, 121-123,
128, 138 *(bottom)*;

John Cafaro, 36 *(bottom)*, 37;

Citywide Photographers, 50, 104 *(bottom)*;

Martha Cooper, 130-131;

D. James Dee, 88, 99, 124 *(top)*;

William Dellenback, 28 *(bottom)*,
29, 34, 51, 120 *(top)*;

William Drescher, 107 *(bottom)*,
112, 125, 127 *(top)*, 133, back cover;

Mindy Gross, 106;

Helga Studios, 11, 22-23;

Jonathan Holstein, 46 *(top)*, 52;

Claus Mroczynski, 21 *(left)*, 24-25, 31, 35,
36 *(top)*, 39 *(bottom)*, 41-43, 46 *(bottom)*,
47, 48 *(bottom)*, 49, 53, 54 *(left)*, 60 *(top)*,
61, 66 *(top)*, 67, 69, 70-71 *(top)*, 70
(bottom), 72-73, 74 *(bottom left)*, 75, 78
(bottom), 84-87, 93, 94 *(bottom)*, 95, 98
(left), 101, 107 *(top)*, 110-111, 113-114, 116,
120 *(bottom)*, 136 *(bottom)*, 137, 141;

National Air and Space Museum, 81 *(top
left, bottom left, top right, center left,
bottom left)*;

National Museum of the American Indian,
Photo #39489 32 *(top)*, #7930 32,
(center), #4763 60 *(bottom)*;

S. Rebsamen, 32 *(bottom)*;

Ann Sanchez, 16 *(bottom)*;

Alan Schindler, 62;

Dan Schlapbach, 66 *(bottom)*, 98 *(right)*,
104 *(top)*, 105;

Bradley Smith, 16 *(top and middle)*, 17;

Gary M. Valant, 80, 81

Sarah Wells, front cover, 20, 30 *(right)*,
33, 44 *(bottom left)*, 57, 65, 71 *(bottom)*, 76,
78 *(top)*, 89, 92, 117 *(bottom)*, 136 *(top)*,
138 *(top)*, 139;

Smithsonian Institution, catalog # 378361,
44 *(center)*

U.S. Air Force Museum, 80, 81 *(top right,
center right)*

Jonathan Williams, 97;

Leon C. Yost, 10, 14-15.